Thomas Cook

TRAVELLERS

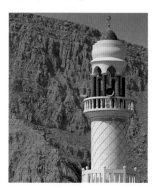

OMAN

DIANA DARKE

Written and updated by Diana Darke
Original photography by Diana Darke

Published by Thomas Cook Publishing
A division of Thomas Cook Tour Operations Limited.
Company registration no. 3772199 England
The Thomas Cook Business Park, Unit 9, Coningsby Road,
Peterborough PE3 8SB, United Kingdom
Email: books@thomascook.com, Tel: + 44 (0) 1733 416477
www.thomascookpublishing.com

Produced by Cambridge Publishing Management Limited
Burr Elm Court, Main Street, Caldecote CB23 7NU

ISBN: 978-1-84848-152-7

First edition © 2007 Thomas Cook Publishing
This second edition © 2009
Text © Thomas Cook Publishing
Maps © Thomas Cook Publishing/PCGraphics (UK) Limited

Project Editor: Adam Royal
Series Editor: Maisie Fitzpatrick
Production/DTP: Steven Collins

Printed and bound in Italy by Printer Trento

Cover photography: Front L-R: © Cubo Images SRL/Alamy; © Cipriani
Settimio/4Corners Images; © Tom Till/Alamy. Back: © Image State/Alamy

Contents

Introduction

Refreshingly different from other holiday destinations, the Sultanate of Oman is the oldest independent state in the Arabian Gulf. Despite the pressures of modernisation and globalisation, it retains a strong sense of identity and its own distinct culture. After the Portuguese were forced out in 1650, the country kept itself unusually isolated and aloof from foreign influences, and was ruled by a highly traditional feudal system.

All this changed in 1970 when the current Sultan, Qaboos Bin Said, ousted his father in a bloodless coup and began very carefully and gradually to open everything up. Using money from the newly discovered oil fields, he embarked on a series of economic reforms and invested for the first time in health, welfare and education. He remains a popular ruler today, a benign autocrat whose decisions are final but always made in the best interests of his country.

Oil and gas production began in 1967, but Oman has successfully followed a policy of slowly reducing dependence on oil revenues, so that now oil accounts for just over half of government income. Inflation has shot up to 12 per cent, a result of the surge in global food prices. Economic diversification is being achieved through developing the ports of Sohar and Salalah, natural gas, information and communications technology, fisheries, manufacturing, and the expansion of tourism through the steady increase in tourist facilities and top-quality hotels. In the 1970s and 1980s, foreign visitors to the Sultanate were tightly controlled and a No Objection Certificate had to be obtained before entry was permitted. This was issued only to visiting businesspeople or to expatriate workers with a pre-arranged job inside the country.

A policy of Omanisation has been followed since the 1980s, with the aim of gradually replacing immigrant workers, many of whom are from the Indian subcontinent, with Omani nationals, to ensure there will be jobs for the growing numbers of young Omanis, and to prepare the country for life post-oil.

While there is no official state religion, most Omanis are Ibadhi Muslims. Ibadhism is an early traditional sect created as a result of one of the first schisms of Islam. There is no sign here of militant Islamist violence of the type that so many Arab countries suffer from. Historically, Oman and the UK have had excellent bilateral relations, often conducting joint military exercises, and Oman also enjoys a free trade agreement with the USA.

TV and radio stations are government controlled but the go-ahead has been given for privately owned Omani stations. Satellite dishes are permitted, but the government reserves the right to censor publications for political or cultural reasons.

Life expectancy for men is 73 years and for women 76 years, and the World Health Organization (WHO) rate Oman's National Health Service as one of the best in the world. There are a number of well-equipped private hospitals and clinics.

This unusual combination in the Arab world – a stable political situation, top-quality tourist facilities, guaranteed sunshine and excellent health care – provides the perfect environment for high-class tourism to flourish. Yet what Oman offers over and above this is a glimpse into the old Arabia, unspoiled and traditional, with its wild and spectacular mountain scenery and forts of the interior, its empty deserts, and its largely untouched coastline and beaches.

Introduction

A typical Omani blend of coast and mountain scenery

The land

More than anything else, Oman's history has been dictated by its geography. Located in a strategic hot spot at the entrance to the Arabian/Persian Gulf, the country straddles a crossroads of natural trade and communication routes. It has 1,700km (1,056 miles) of coastline and overlooks three seas: the Gulf of Oman, the Arabian Sea and the Arabian Gulf. With water dominating its northern and eastern borders, the country has long been a maritime state with a history of navigation and trade. All its major cities are on the coast.

However, behind the coastal plain is another world – 82 per cent desert with the remainder forming mountain ranges and wadis (river valleys). This extraordinary split was reflected in local terminology until as late as the 1960s, when the country was called Muscat and Oman, where Muscat referred to the coast, and Oman referred to the interior. Hence, someone heading into the interior from the coast would say 'I am going to Oman'. This geographical split resulted in much friction between the peoples of the coast and the interior, with their conflicting needs and preoccupations. At many times in the country's history, the interior was ruled entirely separately from the coastal cities and plains.

With an area of 309,500sq km (119,500sq miles), Oman equates in size roughly with Great Britain, and is the second-largest country in the Arabian Peninsula after Saudi Arabia,

bigger than Syria, Jordan and Lebanon combined. The name 'Oman' is thought to mean 'the abode' or 'the land', although other local traditions hold that it was named after 'Uman Ibn Qahtan, Oman's first legendary inhabitant. The land borders are with Saudi Arabia and the United Arab Emirates to the west, and with Yemen to the south.

Topography

Oman has been dissected by early Arab geographers and labelled to resemble the human body. The head is thought of as the Musandam Peninsula (in Arabic, Ru'us Al-Jibaal – Heads of the Mountains), while the backbone or spine is the Hajar mountain range. The stretch running alongside the mountains from Buraimi to Nizwa resembles the back (Al-Dhahirah), and the coastal plain extending down to Muscat is the stomach or underbelly

(Al-Batinah). South of this is the region known as the Sharqiyah (Eastern Province), which is the bulge on the map from Muscat south to Sur and its hinterland. Below this is Jaa'lan (named after its inhabitants, known as the 'People of the Water Beetle'), which is the eastern coastal stretch from Sur to Masirah Island, Oman's largest island. Still further south is the vast gravel desert of Jiddat Al-Harasis, a seemingly endless 800km (500 miles), reaching the Mountains of the Moon, and the scenic Dhofar province with Salalah as its capital. Immediately north of Dhofar, the gravelly plains of the Nejd merge into the perilous Empty Quarter (Ar-Rub' Al-Khaali) where no roads lead.

Behind the Batinah coastal plain lies a series of mountain ranges running parallel to the coast that represent Oman's most stunning and dramatic scenery. The country's highest mountain, Jebel Shams, stands here at 3,048m (10,000ft) within the Jebel Akhdar (Green Mountain) range. The country has no lakes, but in between the mountain ranges are fertile wadis supplied with water by numerous wells and springs and by rainfall that averages 20–25cm (8–10in) a year, higher than that of the Arabian Peninsula generally.

The volcanic mountains of Oman's interior make a lasting impression

Climate

Oman's climate is at its best from late October to early March, with temperatures averaging 30°C (85°F). The coolest months are January and February when average temperatures drop to 25°C (75°F). From March onwards, temperatures start climbing, getting up into the 40s (°C) (100s in °F) in June and July, the hottest months, and with humidity approaching 100 per cent. Temperatures can also fluctuate greatly, so that in July it can reach 48°C (120°F) in the northern oil-producing desert areas around Fahud, but only 13°C (55°F) in the mountains. Near the summit of Jebel Shams, where night-time temperatures are often below freezing point, it can even snow in the winter months. Hailstorms are another winter phenomenon, sometimes falling so hard that people are injured and taken to hospital, livestock are killed and crops damaged. Rains may occur any time between October and March in northern Oman, and it is not unusual for them to be so torrential that wadis are in flood, causing havoc on the Muscat–Nizwa highway where it is crossed by many wadis running off the Jebel Akhdar.

The climate of Dhofar in southern Oman is completely different, keeping around 33°C (90°F). Then from mid-June until mid-September, the monsoon rains arrive, producing a fabulously green landscape. As a result, Salalah is at its most beautiful in September and early October, definitely the best time to visit. By November, the greenery has disappeared again.

Extreme temperatures in the desert

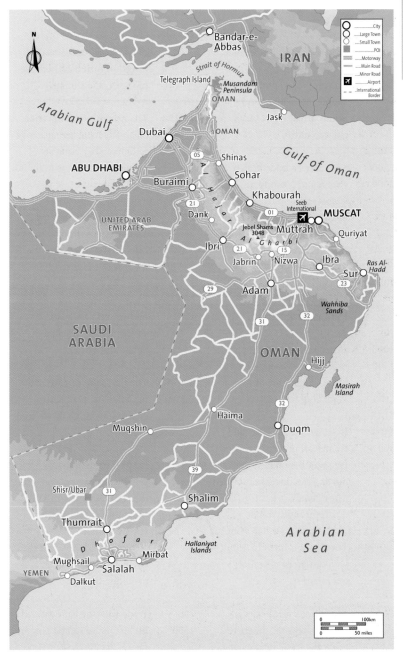

History

3000 BC First references to Oman as Magan, naming it as the source of Mesopotamian copper. Settlement and tombs at Bat show Magan's great wealth.

2500–2000 BC Rich copper trade between Oman and Mesopotamia. Camel is domesticated as a beast of burden. Wadi Jizzi sites and tombs are known as the Umm Al-Nar period.

2000 BC Oman's trading power is eclipsed by the rise of Dilmun (Bahrain).

2000–1300 BC Oman's main trading partner is Dilmun. Sites at Samad and Ras Al-Junayz are known as Wadi Suq period.

1300–300 BC Iron Age sites at Ubar and Khor Rori in the south, and Lizq and Bawshar in the north. Frankincense is traded using camel caravans to the north through Arabia.

c.1000 BC The Persians introduce the *falaj* system of irrigation to Oman.

24 BC The Roman army tries to march across the desert to reach the frankincense lands of southern Arabia but it is forced to turn back because of the hostile climate.

AD 130 The Adnani (Ghafiri) tribes, originally from Yemen, settle in Oman after years of wandering in Saudi Arabia's Nejd desert.

200 The Azdite (Hinawi) tribes, also originally from Yemen, migrate to Oman after the Maarib Dam bursts.

200–400 Sassanians from Iran are in power, and Sassanian governors are installed in Sohar and Rustaq.

400–500 The first signs of Christianity in Oman, with an early Nestorian church discovered in Sohar.

630 Prophet Muhammad's general arrives and converts the country to Islam. After Muhammad's death, the Hinawis follow Ibadhi puritanical Islam, while the Ghafiris follow Sunni orthodox Islam.

700–1500 Trade with the Far East and India; Omani capital Nizwa, then Sohar, then Qalhat.

1507	The Portuguese under Albuquerque arrive in Oman, burning Omani fishing fleets and pillaging coastal towns.
1650	The end of 150 years of Portuguese domination. Oman is independent from this point onwards.
1749	Founding of Al Bu Said dynasty (of whom Sultan Qaboos is the current representative). The capital moves to Muscat.
1750–1800	Oman is wooed by Britain and France, both seeking political alliance and favour with Oman.
1800–1900	The Omani empire expands to include Zanzibar and Mombasa on Africa's east coast and parts of the Indian subcontinent. Anti-slavery treaties and friendship, commerce and navigation treaties are made with Britain.
1913	The control of the country splits. The allegiance of inland tribes is lost because of the sultans' preoccupation with maritime and overseas interests.
1950s	The Jebel wars. Qaboos' father Said regains control of the interior. He is supported by the British who want to prospect for oil.
1964	The Shell oil company discovers oil in commercial quantities in Oman.
1967	Britain withdraws from Aden in South Yemen. The Russians and Chinese move in to fill the vacuum and launch the Dhofar War, aiming to overthrow the Sultan and take control of Oman and the Straits of Hormuz. The war finally ends in 1975 with the help of the British.
1970	Qaboos leads a bloodless coup against his father and comes to power aged 30.
1970–2009	Qaboos embarks upon the modernisation of Omani infrastructure using oil revenues, and initiates a gradual diversification away from oil towards manufacturing, shipping and tourism.
2009	An historic free-trade agreement with the US takes effect, eliminating tariff barriers on all consumer and industrial products.

Tribal structure

Oman is one of the few places in the Arab world where the tribal system continues to matter and to remain strong, although its force has inevitably waned over the last 20 years or so.

The Omani people

Originally, native Omanis lived in the interior, not on the coast, and their tribal allegiances were of paramount importance. Omanis make up about 80 per cent of the population and are ethnic Arabs, descendants either of the Azd tribe that came from Yemen, or the Adnan tribe from the Nejd in Saudi Arabia. On the coast, the population is predominantly made up of merchant classes known as the Baharina, originally of Persian ancestry and Shi'ite, together with the Khojas or Hyderabadis who are Shi'ites of Indian origin. Trading links within their families flourished up and down the Gulf, with uncles, brothers and cousins handling business in Bahrain, Kuwait, Dubai and Qatar. The Beluch is the other tribal group living on the coast that is not native to Oman but originally from an area between Iran, Afghanistan and Pakistan. Zanzibari Omanis, with darker skin and bigger eyes testifying to their East African origins, are also found more on the coast than in the interior.

The Sheikhs and the tribal system

Tribal allegiance is through birth, not through marriage, which is why the ideal is to marry within your own tribe. Each main tribe has its paramount or senior Sheikh who is consolidated in this position by the Sultan, although not appointed by him. The Sheikh acquires his position through the consensus of the tribe, not by hereditary succession and not by appointment of the Sultan. If the tribe commits an offence, the Sheikh is held responsible. The Sheikh also

ZANZIBAR

In the 19th century, Oman extended its trading empire to East Africa, principally the island of Zanzibar, with slaves as the chief commodity. Sultan Said even moved to Zanzibar, and rarely visited Oman. When he died, one son ruled in Zanzibar, the other in Muscat – a split that was formalised in 1861 when Muscat renounced all claims on Zanzibar. In 1890, Zanzibar was parcelled out to Britain as a protectorate. After the Zanzibari revolution in 1963, large numbers of Zanzibari Omanis fled to Oman, which they considered their homeland, settling mainly in the Sharqiyah (Eastern Province).

Each sheikh needed his own fortifications to defend his territory

receives the traditional tribal tribute from the Sultan. Interesting tensions can arise between the Sheikh and the nearest *wali* (local governor), which are resolved according to how the Sheikh's power stacks up against the *wali's* influence. The Sheikh, like the *wali*, conducts his business with the Sultan via the Minister of Interior.

Ghafiri/Hinawi split

The Ghafiri/Hinawi split is the most major divide in Oman's tribes, the difference going back to the two major original tribes, the Azdis and the Adnanis. The split appeared when the two quarrelled over the succession to the Imamate (area ruled by the imam), where the Azdis favoured a Ghafiri (and Sunni) candidate and the Adnanis favoured a Hinawi (and Ibadhi) candidate. Tribal affiliations are still important today, but loyalties continue to fluctuate, and memories linger on of recent blood feuds. Even now, rivalries can still flare up from time to time, rather like rivalries between local clubs or even football teams.

Politics

The Sultanate of Oman is a monarchy headed since 1970 by Sultan Qaboos Bin Said. There are no political parties but the Sultan is helped in his decision making by a Consultative Council (Arabic Majlis Ash-Shura) with 82 elected members.

Government structure

In 1996, Sultan Qaboos introduced Oman's first written constitution, known as the Basic Law. This law established a system for the succession on Qaboos' death (he is not married and has no heir), and set out his own powers and those of his ministers and councils. It also created a 40-member upper chamber called the State Council (Arabic Majlis Ad-Dawla) with appointed members to complement the elected Majlis Ash-Shura. Four women were appointed to the Majlis Ad-Dawla in 1997, and five more in 2003. Two women were also elected to the Majlis Ash-Shura in 2003 when the Sultan extended the vote to all Omanis over 21 in a major step towards democracy. The councils' powers are limited but slowly growing. The Sultan himself still has responsibility for new legislation and for making public appointments. He also holds the portfolios of Minister of Defence, Minister of Finance and of Foreign Policy.

There are currently three women cabinet ministers.

International relations

The only memberships of international groups or organisations that Oman holds are of the Gulf Cooperation Council (GCC), the Organisation of the Islamic Council (OIC), the Arab League and the United Nations (UN). Oman has good relations with its GCC partners (Bahrain, Qatar, Saudi Arabia, United Arab Emirates and Kuwait), and has good working relations with Iran.

The UK and Oman have strong bilateral relations, often conducting joint military exercises. Oman is also a long-standing US ally, and there is a free trade agreement between the two countries.

On the Middle East question, Oman supports the Arab position of suspending all links with Israel until peace talks resume. The Roadmap for Peace is viewed as very important, and the country supports efforts by the Quartet (the USA, the EU, the UN and Russia) to help move the process forward to reach final settlement.

Human rights

The Basic Law sets out rights to an independent judiciary and to freedom of speech and press. However, in practice the media exercises rigorous self-censorship and the internet is monitored. Oman retains the death penalty but has not invoked it for several years.

EARLY FOREIGN POLICY

When Sultan Qaboos came to power in 1970, Oman had diplomatic relations with just two countries, Britain and India. His father, Said Bin Taimur, had thought membership of such bodies as the UN to be unnecessary and pointless. He felt this view justified when the UN's first regional act was to condemn Britain as the aggressor for sending British troops, at the Sultan's request, to help fight against the Imamate revolution in 1957. The old Sultan trusted none of his Arab neighbours, with the exception of Sheikh Zayed of Abu Dhabi. Today, Oman has diplomatic relations with over 100 countries, and is a member of the UN and the Gulf Cooperation Council (GCC).

The Sultan's palace on Muscat harbourfront

Culture

Despite its strategic location at the mouth of the Arabian Gulf, the character of Oman is essentially insular, cut off from its neighbours by deserts, mountains or sea. In pre-oil days, the scarcity of its natural resources, such as water and fertile land, meant that only with a great deal of sustained effort could any people, city or district rise above subsistence level. This has had its effect on the Omani personality, which is inward-looking, reserved and self-controlled, yet with a quiet charm. Omanis are never loud or in your face.

Family ties are extremely strong, the bond that holds communities together, and this is reflected in the use of prefixes in names: Aal means 'family of'; Bin or Ibn means 'son of'; bint means 'daughter of'; and Bani or Beni means 'tribe of'. Lineage is patriarchal and names can extend several generations to clarify. The present Sultan's full name is therefore Qaboos Bin Said Bin Taimur Bin Faisal Bin Turki Bin Said Bin Sultan Bin Ahmad Al Said.

The household is run by the husband/father who has taken a wife to live with him. Islam permits up to four wives, provided that all wives are treated equally. In practice, most Omanis prefer to remain monogamous, only remarrying if the first wife turns out to be infertile, for example. Marriage is a civil ceremony in Islam, performed before a *qadi* (judge), where the bride and groom sign a contract before the members of the families. Afterwards, celebrations can go on for days, with separate parties for men and women. The average age for marriage used to be around puberty for young women, but has now risen into the twenties as the Sultan has encouraged women to finish their education and join the public and private sector

ROLE OF WOMEN

In Oman, women have a higher profile in public life than in other countries of the Gulf. More than half of Oman's university students are women, and they take up careers in teaching, medicine and banking. In the Sultan's words (*Omani Yearbook*, 1996):

'Many years ago I said that if the energy, capability and enthusiasm of women were excluded from a country's active life, then that country would be depriving itself of 50% of its genius. I have taken very good care that this should not happen to Oman, and I look forward to the further progress of women in my country with the greatest pleasure and confidence.'

as working professionals before marriage.

Divorce is still rare, despite the widely held belief that all a man has to do is say three times 'I divorce you'. A woman can petition a judge for divorce on grounds of non-support, adultery or impotence. In practice, divorce is not entered into lightly by either party. Family honour is paramount, and an unfaithful wife shames her father and brothers more than her husband.

Oman today is a very young society with over 50 per cent of the population below the age of 20. As a result, the traditions are changing fast, and the challenge for the Sultan will be to preserve a contented youth culture into the 21st century.

Livestock fodder is traded at market

Traditional crafts

The age-old skills that the Omani people developed over the centuries were deeply rooted in their struggle to survive in a harsh environment with limited raw materials at their disposal. They had to build, weave and carve whatever they needed to go about their daily lives; for example, palm fronds were braided and stitched to make baskets, mats, fans and other household items. The technology of a developing society has rendered these traditional crafts all but redundant today, but tourism plays a vital role in maintaining a demand for them.

Weaving and dyeing

Villagers in the interior of the country still weave hair fibres gathered from goats and camels, and wool from sheep to make cloth, blankets and carpets. Spinning used to be done by hand on small spindles, not spinning wheels, after which it was ready for dyeing. Colours came from pigments in local vegetation, and so red was

Traditional Omani chest for sale in Nizwa *souk*

Wood carving decorating a door

made from crushed madder root, purple from shells of murex, yellow from a mix of local plants.

Pottery

Pots were made in Oman from the 3rd millennium BC, and today the craft continues in Bahla in the interior and to a lesser extent in Salalah to the south. Using a foot-driven wheel, the potters bake a variety of earthenware in large mud-brick kilns, including incense burners, bowls, storage jars and coffee pots.

Jewellery

As an essential part of the Omani costume, men, as well as women, wore silver. For example, men carried keys on fine chains, money holders, tweezers in silver cases, toothpicks and ear cleaners on silver chains, and belts to hold their *khanjar* or curved dagger. Sadly, much of the antique silver was melted down before traders realised its worth, so now very little genuine antique silver is left to buy. Women's head pieces with decorative coins or Maria Theresa dollars used to be so heavy that they could only really be worn when seated, such as on special occasions like weddings. There were regional variations in style between the different provinces, and Dhofari bracelets, for example, had coral beads and spiky silver washers threaded onto elastic. Gold jewellery is much more delicate, with filigree earrings, nose rings, necklaces and pendants. Both gold and silver were imported from India.

THE DYEING OUT OF INDIGO

What we think of as black in the outer garment of women (*abayah*) is in fact indigo, traditionally made from the plant called 'neel'. Neel was picked and soaked in water for two days, the dye in the leaves sinking to the bottom. The water was poured off and the residue left to dry for two or three days, then cut into small tablets to be sold to the professional dyers in the towns. Before modern drugs arrived, indigo was also used medicinally to soothe skin diseases and heal wounds such as the umbilical cord on a newborn baby. Other Arab countries, such as Egypt, still use gentian violet for these types of wounds as it has drying as well as healing properties.

Festivals and events

As a conservative Muslim country, Oman's major annual celebrations are the Islamic festivals, known as Eids *in Arabic. Friday is the holy day of the week when souks (markets), offices and banks are closed. The two main Islamic festivals are the Eid Al-Adha and the Eid Al-Fitr, which follows the end of Ramadan. Shops and offices close for three or four days' holiday during both events, which are joyous, colourful occasions with lots of eating.*

Ramadan

The Muslim month of fasting that lasts for 30 days is looked forward to and enjoyed by Omanis because it is a time for visiting friends and family after dark, when social activity tendsto go on into the small hours. As a result, everything starts late in the morning with offices and shops opening later and closing earlier. The Koran states that all Muslims must abstain from food, drink, smoking and sexual intercourse (all the bodily pleasures) during daylight hours. Younger children, pregnant women, the old and sick and travellers on long journeys are the only ones exempt. Daylight is defined as when you can distinguish a black thread from a white thread. Non-Muslims are also affected because the law forbids anyone to be seen eating, drinking or smoking in public during the day. Restaurants are therefore mostly closed except in the big tourist hotels where a screened-off area is kept for non-Muslims. Bars are also closed, and hotels are not allowed to serve alcohol publicly, although consumption in the privacy of your hotel room is fine.

THE ISLAMIC CALENDAR

As a lunar calendar, the Islamic calendar is based on the cycles of the moon, making the Muslim year 11 days shorter than the Gregorian calendar. This is why the Muslim festivals keep moving backwards each year by 11 days in our calendar, although they of course remain fixed in the Islamic calendar. Ramadan becomes particularly hard when it falls over the summer as it will do in the coming years. In 2009, Ramadan will begin on 21 August. The end of each of the 12 Muslim months is determined by the sighting of the new moon, and hence exact dates are hard to predict. Geography also comes into it, as the new moon is spotted in different countries at different times, so the exact date can vary by up to three days depending on the country you are in. Saudi Arabia, as the guardian of the holy sites of Mecca and Medina, likes to take the lead and has been known to send up a helicopter to make sure the new moon is spotted on the day it prefers. Oman, not wanting to appear subservient, generally goes for a different day on principle.

National Day

This is the only public holiday that Omanis celebrate on a fixed day, 18 November, coinciding with Sultan Qaboos' birthday. There are always fabulous firework displays and camel races at Seeb.

Omani celebrations are mostly Islamic in origin, with mosques such as this one in Fiqain playing an important role in daily life

Highlights

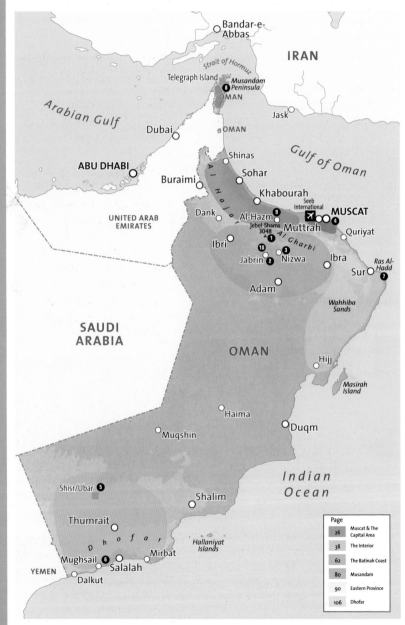

IRAN

Bandar-e-Abbas

Strait of Hormuz

Telegraph Island

Musandam Peninsula

8 OMAN

Jask

Arabian Gulf

OMAN

Gulf of Oman

Dubai

Shinas

ABU DHABI

Buraimi

Sohar

Khabourah

Seeb International

MUSCAT

Dank

Al-Hazm **9**

Al Hajar

Muttrah **4**

Quriyat

Jebel Shams 3048 **1**

Al Gharbi

Ibri

10

3

Ibra

Ras Al-Hadd

Jabrin **2**

Nizwa

Sur **7**

UNITED ARAB EMIRATES

Adam

Wahhiba Sands

SAUDI ARABIA

OMAN

Hijj

Masirah Island

Haima

Duqm

Muqshin

Shisr/Ubar **5**

Indian Ocean

Shalim

Thumrait

Dhofar

Hallaniyat Islands

Mughsail **6**

Mirbat

YEMEN

Salalah

Dalkut

Page	
26	Muscat & The Capital Area
38	The Interior
62	The Batinah Coast
80	Musandam
90	Eastern Province
106	Dhofar

① Explore the dramatic scenery of the Jebel Akhdar mountains by four-wheel drive to reach Oman's Grand Canyon, the Wadi Nakhr (*see p47*).

② Marvel at the magnificent painted ceilings and decorations inside the restored 17th-century Jabrin fort (*see p52*).

③ Stroll around the fort and *souks* (markets) at Nizwa looking for traditional crafts, and eye up the next-door livestock markets with their camels and goats (*see p48*).

④ Admire the natural harbour setting of Muscat flanked by its pair of Portuguese forts, and walk around the old town with its restored walls and gates and 19th-century museum houses (*see p30*).

⑤ Visit the remote ruins of Shisr, the evocative site on the edge of the Empty Quarter, thought to be the elusive ancient Ubar, Atlantis of the Sands (*see p118*).

⑥ Drive the amazingly engineered road west from Salalah towards the Yemeni border to see the frankincense trees on the hillsides and the blowholes at Mughsail (*see p116*).

⑦ Watch turtles hatch at dawn on the beaches of Ras Al-Hadd (*see p99*).

⑧ Take a boat trip, accompanied by leaping dolphins, to Telegraph Island in the Musandam through landscapes of mountainous fjords (*see p84*).

⑨ Get lost in the maze of rooms and corridors in the magnificent 18th-century fort of Al-Hazm (*see p68*).

⑩ Camp at full moon in the spectacular well-watered wadis of the Jebel Akhdar, such as Wadi Fidda, Wadi Tannuf and Wadi Abyadh (*see pp57, 60 & 74*).

Richly painted ceiling at Jabrin fort

Suggested itineraries

You can get a flavour of what Oman has to offer in a long weekend, but to see it properly you need at least two weeks so that you can visit the south as well. If you go to Dhofar in the south, make sure it is during September/October so that you see it at its best after the monsoon has turned the hillsides green. Four-wheel drive is not required for any of the itineraries described below unless expressly stated.

Long weekend

Day 1	Fly into Muscat.
Day 2	Visit Old Muscat with its museums, and the harbour area with the forts of Jelali and Merani.
Day 3	Take a day trip to the interior to visit Nizwa fort and *souk* (market) and the forts of Bahla and Jabrin.
Day 4	Spend a day at Oman Dive Center (*see p161*).
Day 5	Return flight.

One week

Day 1	Fly into Muscat.
Day 2	Visit Muscat old town; Bait Fransa, Jalali and Merani forts; Bait Al-Zubair; Muttrah's seafront and *souk* (market); and Bawshar's ruined and restored forts. Stay overnight at Muscat.
Day 3	Visit Bait Ar-Radaida fort; Nizwa fort and restored *souk* (market); Fiqain's fortified house. Stay overnight at Nizwa.
Day 4	Go to see Tannuf's ruins; Hamra's old town; Misfah mountain village; Wadi Ghul. Four-wheel drive the ascent to Jebel Akhdar. Stay overnight in Nizwa/Bahla.
Day 5	Visit Bahla town, fort and *souk* (market); Jabrin palace; Sulaif; Wadi Dank scenery. Stay overnight at Nizwa/Bahla.
Day 6	Explore Fanja's old citadel; Bait Na'man's fortified house; Nakhl fort; Ain Ath-Thawra hot springs. Stay overnight at Sawadi.
Day 7	Visit Rustaq town and fort; Al Hazm fort; Barka fort. Stay overnight at Muscat.
Day 8	Return flight.

Two weeks

An extra week will allow you to do the one-week itinerary (*see above*) and add on a flight to Khasab in Musandam and spend two days (two or three nights) exploring the mountains and fjords. A four-wheel drive is required.

You can then spend two nights in Sur (no four-wheel drive required), visiting Bidbid fort, Ibra's ruined quarter, Al Mudayrib, then Sur itself, Al Ayjah town and Qalhat ruined city. If you have a four-wheel drive vehicle, you can return to Muscat from Sur along the coast, taking in Wadi Dayqah and Tiwi.

Three weeks

A third week allows you to extend the two-week itinerary (*see above*) and fly south to Salalah and spend a leisurely three days (three/four nights) visiting the main sights of Sumharam, Khor Rori, Mirbat, Mughsail, Wadi Dirbat, Shisr and the Pools of Ayoun. Then fly

SELF-DRIVE CAR HIRE

The road network in Oman is now extremely good; a far cry from the 1960s when there was only 416km (260 miles) of tarmac road. Traffic drives on the right and is generally extremely well behaved by Middle Eastern standards. Therefore, self-drive car hire is not at all daunting and is to be recommended. Petrol is cheap and drivers need to be over 21. There are no railways in Oman, but there is an efficient coach network. However, to follow the above itineraries by coach would require more time than has been allowed, as the routes and timings are geared to car travel.

back to Muscat and allow two to three days (two/three nights) for exploring Sohar itself and its hinterland, with copper mines in Wadi Jizzi, the Arja ziggurat (ancient temple towers) and the medieval stronghold of Hawra Burghah.

Old Ibra in the Sharqiyah province

Muscat

A European traveller's account of Muscat in the 1830s runs (Oman in history, 1995):

'With all its barrenness and unpromising appearance, such is the advantage of position enjoyed by Muscat, commanding, as it does, the entrance to the Persian Gulf, that its harbours are filled with vessels from all ports of the East, and the busy din of commerce constantly enlivens its streets. In few parts of the world can the necessaries, nay even the luxuries, of life, be obtained in greater profusion.'

Oman's capital city since 1749, Muscat's harbour was always its chief attribute. The very name Muscat means 'Place of Anchorage' in Arabic, and with the ring of mountains protecting it from the inland side, Muscat was always a safe haven for shipping. Archaeological evidence suggests the city was founded some 900 years before Islam, probably by Yemeni tribes. The sea has always played a vital part in shaping the history of Oman in general and of Muscat in particular. The Portuguese left their mark in the 16th century, building the two forts Merani and Jalali to guard the harbour. They made

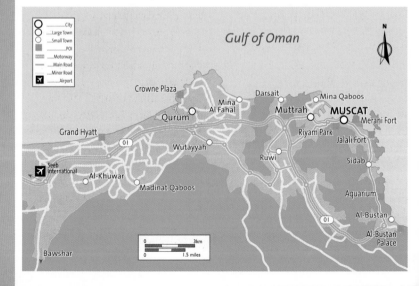

Impressive gateway to Muscat's old walled city

Muscat their base from which to control the trade routes to India, and their admiral, Alfonso de Albuquerque, described Muscat as 'a large and populous city – there are orchards, gardens and palm groves with pools for watering them by means of wooden engines – it is a very elegant town with very fine houses'.

Before modernisation in 1970, Muscat could only be reached with difficulty from inland. Mountain passes had to be crossed on foot or by donkey, and the city itself was ringed by a high wall and deep moat. The richer residents lived within the wall in spacious and elegant houses of clay, while the poor lived outside the walls in simple wooden huts.

Today, it is hard to imagine that in 1970 there was only one tarmac road in Muscat, from the old city to the airport at Bait Al-Falaj. Now, the road network is established with an efficient system of dual carriageways and flyovers, all guiding you through the beautifully manicured landscaping of the Capital Area. Muscat remains an elegant political capital. Spotlessly clean and well maintained, it is often dubbed 'the jewel of Arabia' by foreign media.

Natural History Museum

Scattered in the suburbs of Ruwi and Madinat Qaboos there are some interesting museums, not often visited. Beside the Ministry of Culture and National Heritage in Khuwair, this museum shows the wildlife of the country, with an impressive collection of skeletons in its unique Whale Hall.
Al Wazarat Street. Tel: 24 604957. Open: Sat–Thur 9.30am–1.30pm. Admission charge.

Oman Museum

The Oman Museum is tucked away on a hillside behind the Ministry of Information overlooking Madinat Qaboos, perhaps the most worthwhile of all Muttrah's museums.

The carefully arranged displays in this treasure trove take you through Oman's earliest history from the Stone Age, covering in some detail the copper mining and the frankincense trade.
Al Alam Street. Tel: 24 600946. Open: Sat–Wed 8am–2.30pm. Closed: Thur & Fri. Admission charge.

Sultan's Armed Forces Museum

Set in the gardens of the white Bait Al-Falaj fort, this impressive museum

---

MUSCAT GRAPE

Known locally as *ghareeb al-wadi*, the famous Muscat grape is still grown in places such as Wadi Mistal. Small and bitter, it is not very good for eating, but it is believed that the Portuguese took the vine plants home with them to make Muscadet wine.

Merani fort with the modern mosque in front

details Oman's military history from the Portuguese occupation to the Dhofar War.
Al Mujamma Street, Ruwi. Tel: 24 312642 Open: Sat–Thur 8am–1.30pm. Admission charge.

JALALI AND MERANI FORTS

Until the last 50 years or so, the usual approach to Muscat was by sea, the most impressive first sighting by far, with the two 16th-century Portuguese-built forts of Jalali and Merani guarding either side of the compact harbour. Before the Portuguese favoured it as their main entrepôt, Muscat had only been a small trading post. Portuguese domination, however, lasted less than 30 years, and when the Omanis re-conquered Muscat in 1650, the last of their struggles in the area, it spelled

SUNSET DHOW CRUISES

The best way to see Muscat from the sea is to take one of the sunset dhow (traditional Omani wooden boat) cruises from the Inshirah Restaurant on the corniche between Muscat and Muttrah. The dhows spend around an hour cruising along the coastal bays of Muscat.

the end of Portuguese colonialism in the Gulf.

Jalali: recent jail

Originally named San Joao and Fort Capitan, the Portuguese completed the Jalali and Merani forts around 1587.

Neither fort is open to the general public, but visiting heads of state, royalty and VIPs can be shown around Jalali, now a museum of Omani heritage and culture, by special arrangement.

Jalali was Oman's main jail until recently, and it still has a formidable air about it. Ringed by a high wall, it is accessible only from the harbour side via a steep flight of steps or by the VIP lift. It is still in use as a garrison for Omani troops. Inside, one of the finest rooms is the long wooden beamed and floored gallery of cannons, with cannon slits trained onto the harbour.

Jalali fort dominates Muscat's harbour

Walk: Old Muscat

A half-day should be allowed for this walk, to include the time spent souvenir shopping in Bait Muzna Gallery and looking inside the museums. The walk would be better in the morning when the museums are open (after 9am) and before the heat has built up, as there is virtually no shade.

The total distance is around 1km (²/₃ mile). Start at the roundabout where the Al Alam Palace approach road begins.

1 Al Alam Palace

A jewel of modern Islamic architecture built in the 1970s as Sultan Qaboos' formal palace for official functions, the building is on a modest scale right on the waterfront. It is not open to the public, but can be observed most closely from its own approach road, surprisingly free of guards. Its upper section is in striking blue and gold colours with tall pointed arches, topped with an elaborate frieze. There are formal gardens at the front and a semi-circular garden at the back that leads directly onto the harbour. When illuminated at night, it looks like a magical Aladdin's palace.

From the roundabout in front of the

Map legend:
- ☆ ...Start of Walk
- ▣ ...POI
- ➕ ...Hospital

AL MERANI ST

Mathaib Gate

ASH SHUHADA ST

Fort Merani

ASH SHUHADA ST

Muscat Bay

Fort Jalali

Khor Mosque

Bait Graiza

❷

AS SULTAN TAIMUR ST

Palace Banqueting Hall

Al Alam Palace ❶

Site of former British Consulate

AL BAB AL KABIR ST

Bait Nadir

AL ALAM ST

Bab Kabir

❸

Bait Fransa

HARAT DAKHIL

➕

HARAT WALJAT

Kabritta Tower

Saghir Gate

AS SULTAN FAISAL ST

Bait Al Zubair ❹

❺ Bait Muzna Gallery

Ali Musa Mosque

AS SULTAN TURKI ST

BAB WALJAT ST

N

| 0 | | 100 metres |
| 0 | | 100 yards |

ECCENTRIC ELEPHANT

The British Consulate was built around 1880 and used to stand proudly on the waterfront, just 100m (110yds) away from Al Alam Palace, until it was demolished in the 1990s to improve the Sultan's view and to provide more space for additional palace buildings. Muscat in the 1800s must have been a rather eccentric place. A tame lion and ostrich were said to roam the streets, and an elephant regularly ambled over to the British Consulate to collect his daily ration of sugar lumps.

palace, turn right and follow Al Alam St, which runs northwest parallel to the coast. At the intersection, turn right into Al Bab Al Kabir St.

2 Bait Graiza

Built around 1820, this magnificent house was once an embassy, but it cannot be entered now. Its design is typical of Muscat at this time, with the downstairs rooms generally used as storerooms and kitchens, and the upstairs as the family living space. In summer, the favourite sitting area was on the roof.
Double back along Al Bab Al Kabir St, past another old house called Bait Nadir on your left, then take the first left to find Bait Fransa immediately on your left.

3 Bait Fransa (Omani French Museum)

Originally the French Consulate until 1920, the interior is well worth a look, elegantly decorated in black and white.
Tel: 24 736613. Open: Sat–Thur 9am–1pm. Admission charge.

Return now to Al Bab Al Kabir St and turn left. You will pass through Bab Kabir (Big Gate) itself. Cross the main road and continue about 150m (160yds), past a crossroads, and immediately on your right you will find Bait Al Zubair.

4 Bait Al Zubair

Opened in 1998 as an Omani Heritage Museum and Cultural Centre, Bait Al Zubair is set in a renovated historic house, with its own craft shop and coffee shop. Inside are models of dhows, *khanjars* (traditional Omani curved daggers), traditional clothing and weapons, all well labelled and explained.
Tel: 24 736688. Open: Sat–Thur 9am–1pm & 4–7pm. Admission charge. Opposite Bait Al Zubair is Bait Muzna Gallery.

5 Bait Muzna Gallery

This is a traditional Omani villa selling a wide range of local artwork and handicrafts.
www.omanart.com. Open: Sat–Thur 9.30am–1.30pm & 4.30–8pm.

Sultan Qaboos' official residence in Muscat, Al Alam Palace

Arab navigation

Arabs developed the art of astro-navigation, and so most stars have Arab names. The Arabs had three grades of navigator: the lowest was the man who knew coastlines and could follow them safely avoiding reefs and other dangers; second was the man who could cross open water following a direct course until he made his landfall; third and highest was the man called a *mu'allim* (scholar or learned person) who could navigate at all times out of sight of land, from port to port, using only the stars and his knowledge.

Sindbad the sailor

In an attempt to recreate the 9,654km (6,000-mile) voyage of Sindbad the

A superb old ocean-going dhow, rescued and now in Sur

Sailor to China, Tim Severin the British explorer and author set sail in his ship, *The Sohar*, in November 1980. The departure from Muscat harbour took place amid cannon fire and bands playing. There were emotional farewells from every Omani who had been involved in building the remarkable ship in true traditional style, from timbers tied together by coconut rope, then coated with sugar and fish oil to make it watertight.

Completed ahead of schedule, the boat took 165 days to build. Severin was accompanied by a crew of 28, eight of them Omani traditional sailors, all volunteers. All but one of these eight married when they docked in Calcutta, carrying on the historical sailor's tradition of keeping a wife in every port.

For the journey they stowed dried fruit, nuts, dried peas, rice and spices, along with sackfuls of onions and eggs cushioned in sawdust. The bilges exuded hydrogen sulphide gas, reeking of rotten eggs. To mimic the original navigation methods, Severin acquired a 15th-century text written in verse by Ibn Majid, a native of Sur famed for his seafaring skills. His only other navigational aids were a piece

Replica of *The Sohar*, used to recreate Sindbad's voyage to China

of string with a knot and cardboard, and of course the Pole Star. The total journey to China took seven months, with the first stretch from Muscat to Calcutta taking one month.

Ibn Majid and the Portuguese

The Portuguese explorer Vasco da Gama is thought to have employed Ibn Majid, the famous Omani navigator, for the Muscat to Calcutta stretch. For the Portuguese this represented a voyage of discovery, whereas for Ibn Majid it would have been a routine journey. They reached India in 1498 and, in the following 30 years or so, the Portuguese carried out a devastating series of attacks on key strategic points. They secured maritime domination of the Arabian seas thanks to their great organisational skills, strong political and economic direction from their homeland, and religious crusading zeal. On a more down-to-earth level, the Portuguese had superior arms and new, faster ship designs. Their aim was to monopolise trade, in particular, the long-distance luxury trade of the Indian seas. They took Hormuz in 1507, but although they built some forts and bases in the region, their practice was to leave power in the hands of local governments as much as possible and to rule indirectly. This avoided the manpower demands, expense and trouble of a direct European administration. They were finally repulsed from the Gulf in the mid-17th century.

Merani: homely barracks

Merani is today the headquarters of the Muscat Garrison. Virtually invincible, the fort was captured from the Portuguese by the Imam Sultan Bin Saif in 1649 by means of a devious trick. An Indian merchant called Narutem held the contract to supply the fort with all its provisions from the Portuguese commander, Pereira. Narutem had a beautiful daughter whom Pereira wished to marry, but Narutem initially refused as he did not want his Hindu daughter to marry a Christian. As a result, Pereira threatened to take away Narutem's contract and bring about his financial ruin. At this, the cunning Narutem pretended to change his mind, and he asked for a year to prepare for the wedding. At the same time, he persuaded Pereira that the wheat stocks in the fort were old and needed replacing and that the cistern water was foul and required changing. However, Narutem surreptitiously removed the water and wheat supplies but, unbeknown to Pereira, did not replace them. Then he sent word to the Imam Sultan Bin Saif that the fort would not be able to resist a siege for long, whereupon the Imam attacked the fort and expelled the Portuguese forever. *The forts are not open to the public.*

MUTTRAH

Set in its own fine harbour just 3km (1³/₄ miles) west of Muscat, Muttrah has always been regarded as the commercial capital of Oman, with easier access to its hinterland and less hemmed in by mountains than Muscat. The wealthy merchants who controlled the trade here in the 18th century built themselves fine houses with latticed windows and carved doors along the crescent-shaped corniche. Many of these houses still survive and give Muttrah the most impressive harbour frontage to be found anywhere in Oman. At the eastern end, Muttrah fort, still used by the military police, dominates the harbour from its rocky crag, but is out of bounds to the public.

Its commercial activities have given Muttrah a population at least four times that of Muscat, and its *souk* (market) is the biggest and liveliest in the country. The busy modern port of Mina Qaboos now dominates the western side of the bay, although there are still plenty of small fishing boats

Elegant merchant house on Muttrah corniche

and even a few traditional old dhows moored on the eastern side. On the western extremity of the harbour is the Fish Souk, a gleaming white building with open arches facing the sea. Early morning is the best time to come, when the fishermen bring in their fresh catch.

Muttrah Souk (Market)

In Oman's oldest and most complex *souk*, you are immediately transported into a different world, with a maze of alleyways leading off the central lane. Its local name is Souk A'Dhalaam (Market of Shade), so-called because it is fully covered. On offer are various exotica like antique *khanjars* (traditional Omani curved daggers) in silver and gold, carpets, old chests, perfumes, frankincense, traditional clothing, as well as the whole gamut of herbs and spices where the aromas blend with fresh coffee and incense to make a heady cocktail. The *souk* is at its busiest in the evenings.

The main entrance to the souk *is at the traffic lights on the corniche, marked by a golden dome. Open: Sat–Thur 9am–1pm & 4.30–11pm, Fri 4.30–11pm.*

Muttrah fort overlooks the corniche from its rocky outcrop

Drive: Through the Capital Area to Bawshar

The whole of the built-up area around Muscat and Muttrah is known as the Capital Area. This drive will take you through its key parts, ending at the forts in Bawshar on the northern edge.

Half a day should be allowed, including the time spent at the Bawshar forts.

The total distance covered is about 12km (7 1/2 miles).

1 Al-Bustan

The whole bay was called Al-Bustan (The Orchard), and the original village of Al-Bustan was moved to the northern corner of the bay and revamped to make way for Oman's most luxurious hotel, Al-Bustan Palace, which now dominates the pretty rock-hemmed bay.

Follow the coast road to the north, passing a few bays, to reach the Capital Area Yacht Club and Aquarium.

2 Aquarium

Beside the Yacht Club, right on the water's edge, is the Aquarium that belongs to the Ministry of Agriculture and Fisheries. It is open to the public

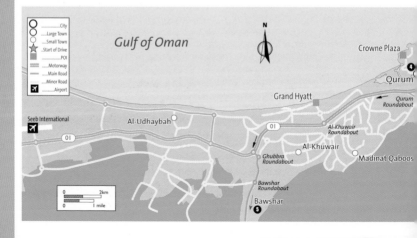

and has a particularly fine collection of turtles in residence.

Open: Sat–Thur 7.30am–2.30pm.

Continue north up the coast, past the fishing village of Sidab on its pretty bay, to reach Muscat proper. Immediately after leaving Muscat, the road follows the corniche and, as it turns west, look out for the car park on your right on the headland.

3 Riyam Park

A good picnic spot is to be found on the headland by the Inshirah (Purple Onion) Restaurant and children's playground. On the other side of the road is the lush Riyam Park, beautifully manicured with colourful flowers and trees for shade.

The coast road continues west to bring you to the distinctive Muttrah corniche fronted by its attractive multistorey merchant houses and busy commercial port of Mina Qaboos at the far end. The road now leaves the coast and skirts

the commercial districts of Ruwi and Darsait. *To your right is the headquarters for PDO (Petroleum Development Oman) and the oil terminal of Mina Al Fahal, after which you reach the Qurum roundabout. Turn right at the roundabout to reach Qurum.*

4 Qurum

Originally just a little fishing village on the southern end of the Batinah, Qurum is now part of the modern sprawl of the Capital Area, and most of the beach hotels are situated along the wide sandy shore, ending in the rocky headland known as Qurum Heights. The marshy estuary with mangrove swamps is now designated a nature reserve. It is in fact the mouth of the Wadi Adai and still floods into the sea after heavy rains.

From the Qurum roundabout, turn right and the road continues west, passing the embassies and ministries to the right, through Al-Khuwair. At the Ghubbra roundabout, turn left and then right, straight over the Bawshar roundabout and uphill to Bawshar. Follow the signposts to Bait Al-Makham.

5 Bawshar

Built around 1900 and restored in 1992, Bait Al-Makham is a fine fortified house.

Open: 7.30am–2.30pm.

From here, a tarmac road runs east through the hills back towards Muscat. Look out for the ruins of two large fortified castles.

Darsait — Mina Qaboos — Mina I Fahal — Muttrah — MUSCAT — Merani Fort — Bait Al Falaj Roundabout — Riyam Park ❸ — Jalali Fort — Mutayyah — Ruwi — Sidab — Ruwi Roundabout — Capital Area Yacht Club — Aquarium ❷ — 01 — Al-Bustan ❶ — Al-Bustan Palace

The interior

Oman's interior (Al-Dakhiliyah) is distinguished by its mountain range, the Jebel Akhdar (Green Mountain), which runs parallel to the coast and cuts off Oman from the sea. This isolation has shaped the character of the Omanis of the interior, making them independent and inward-looking, distanced as they were both literally and historically from the trade and foreign influences prevalent on the coast.

In the interior, tribal allegiances were paramount and the authority of the Imam (the elected head of the Ibadhi sect) was accepted in religion and politics, rather than that of the Sultan, who was seen as too preoccupied with worldly matters of trade and overseas commerce.

The main towns of Nizwa and Bahla offer a wealth of sites for the visitor, and the road network makes it easy to travel around by car. Four-wheel drives are only needed for the ascent of Jebel Shams and for access to remoter wadis. Scenically, the interior is undoubtedly the most beautiful region of Oman.

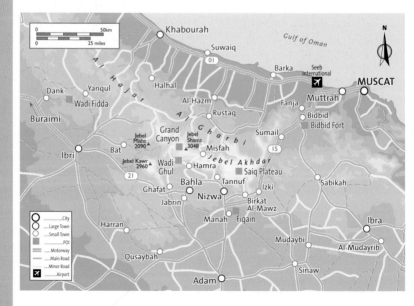

BIDBID

The fort here, rising above the date palms on the very edge of the wide wadi bed, was the first one in Oman to be restored using traditional methods from the original materials of mud, gypsum and straw. Its location is very attractive, with a fine *falaj* (see p42) channel running in front of the main gate and a simple Ibadhi mosque to one side. The fort appears to be permanently locked, and all the rooms are empty.

2km (1¹/4 miles) past the Fanja exit on the main dual carriageway, follow the

THE IMPORTANCE OF TRIBES

Even today, tribal characteristics and traditions continue to matter. The town of Ghafat is still dominated by the Beni Hina tribe, the town of Hamra by the Abriyeen, the towns of Tannuf and Birkat Al-Mawz by the Beni Riyam – and, wherever possible, marriage within the tribe was and still is encouraged. The walled towns were controlled by the ruling sheikh of each tribe, who was elected to his position by consensus. Today, the *wali* or local governor is still likely to be from a local tribe rather than posted in from elsewhere.

The interior

The rugged mountains of the Jebel Akhdar

tarmac road through the village of
Bidbid, then fork left for 1km (²/₃ mile) to
the fort. Allow 30 minutes from Muscat.

FANJA

Heading out from Muscat, Fanja rises
up to the right of the road, an old
walled town on the edge of the
mountains, now all but deserted. After
entering the old gateway, you walk up
the steep escarpment past the 17th-
century cannon to the simple round
fortification towers, one of which, at
the summit, is an unusual oval shape.
The walk to the top takes about
15 minutes, and the views out over
the palm groves and the majestic sweep
of the wadi make it worthwhile.
32km (20 miles) inland along the excellent
dual carriageway from the coast and
Muscat, Fanja is prominently visible to

the right on a high escarpment above the
modern town. Fork off right through
the new villages towards the escarpment
and park at the foot near some shops.
A 5-minute walk uphill brings you to the
old gateway.

SUMAIL GAP

There are around 115 forts or towers
defending this area, such was the
importance of the Sumail Gap, the

Bidbid fort sits on the edge of an oasis

Fanja with its watchtowers overlooking the wadi

most obvious route from Oman's coast to the interior. It is now the course of the main highway from Muscat to Nizwa, and it gradually climbs to a height of 700m (2,300ft). The Sumail Gap is the natural break in the Hajar mountain range, between the vast expanses of limestone rock with their phenomenal geological layering to the north, and the much lower jagged hills that continue to run southwards into the Sharqiyah (Eastern Province).

As is quite common in Oman, Sumail village itself has both an upper (Aliyat) section and lower (Sufelat) section. These sections warred constantly with each other because one was of the Ghafiri tribe and the other of the Hinawi. The *wali* (governor) used to live in the great fort in the lower Ghafiri town until the 1960s. This was the main building of the village that also served as a Koran school, the judge's office and a prison. *60km (37 miles) inland from the airport and coast.*

PERSIAN STEPS

Several paths exist up into the mountains, including the so-called 1,400 Persian Steps, which are cut from the rock to reach the plateau at 2,000m (6,562ft). Locals can walk this path in under two hours, but you will be hard pushed to manage it in four.

The *falaj* system

Oman's complex irrigation system known as the *falaj* is thought to have originated in Persia around 1000 BC and brought to Oman in pre-Islamic times. According to Omani legend, the more colourful explanation is that the Prophet Dawood, father of Sulaiman, came on a flying carpet and ordered his genies to build it. The *falaj* is a channel for conducting water from its source, usually an underground spring, to the fields where irrigation is required. There are

The *falaj* is always well maintained

estimated to be 7,000 *aflaaj* (plural of *falaj*) in Oman today, around half of which flow all year round. Some are said to originate 15m (50ft) underground, while some never go underground at all, and some run a long way, while others are very short. The average length is 3–5km (1³/₄–3 miles).

Omanis distinguish between two types of *falaj*, the *dawoodia* and the *ghail*. The *dawoodia* is built underground and gets its water from the rainfall runoff that collects underground in the subsoil of the mountains. This is generally a more constant supply than the *ghail*, only flowing more strongly at times of heavy rainfall. The *ghail* tends to be smaller and runs overland, collecting water runoff from small, seasonal wadis, which then runs into pools. This type of *falaj* will be dry when there is no rainfall.

For centuries, village life in Oman has been organised around the equitable distribution of water between the palm groves and gardens of different owners. The maintenance of the main canal is the responsibility of the entire village, and each owner pays a share once a year to ensure proper maintenance is carried out.

Falaj Daris, a rare covered *falaj* system in Nizwa

A chief caretaker is appointed by the village, along with a chief maintenance man and a tax collector. Since the *falaj* system works using the natural hydraulic power of gravity, no machinery is required, making it environmentally friendly and economic. The whole management of the system to the common good also instils teamwork and cooperation among the villagers, with each member contributing to the well-being of the other. *Falaj* books used to be kept containing title, sales and accounts of the *aflaaj*, which would have given fascinating glimpses into the hierarchy of a rural community. In many village communities, the *falaj* is still part of the essential way of life, and one of the standard exchanges for a visitor on arrival at a neighbouring village is 'And how are the *aflaaj*?' 'Full, in sha Allah' ('Full, if God wills').

As well as running underground to irrigate the fields and date plantations, some *aflaaj* also ran through forts, such as at Al-Hazm, thereby giving the fort its own private water supply and washing areas. Muslims always wash under running water which is considered far more hygienic than the Western habit of sitting in bath water.

OLDEST *FALAJ*

The town of Izki has what is reputed to be Oman's oldest *falaj*, the Falaj Al-Mulki, which had 370 separate channels in its earliest Persian form. It is still well maintained, and a superb example of a stone-roofed tunnel, some 2m (6^1/$_2$ft) high. Steps lead down to it where it flows about 30cm (12in) deep, set over 3m (10ft) below ground level.

The interior

BIRKAT AL-MAWZ

The town of Birkat Al-Mawz (Pool of Bananas) is inhabited by members of the Beni Riyam, the tribe whose sheikh was the rebel leader in the Jebel War. The sheikh's palace guards the entrance to the Wadi Muaydin, a key route up into the mountains, from where a military road leads up to the Saiq Plateau. Known as Bait Al-Radaidah, the palace was restored in 1999 and opened to the public.

105km (65 miles) from Muscat. Palace open: Sun–Thur 8am–2.30pm. Admission charge.

IZKI

The *wilayet* (governorate) of Izki has 26 villages that have 142 watchtowers between them. The town itself, known for its tribal intrigues, is split into Hinawi clan members (Yemeni from the south), and Ghafiri clan members (Nizari from the Nejd in Saudi Arabia in the north) – the great tribal divide of Oman and source of much civil strife. Intermarriage between the two tribes was taboo until very recently, and their dialects still retain their separate characteristics.

Izki lies along the course of the Wadi Halfayn, one of Oman's great wadis. The wadi is normally dry, but after heavy rain it can be transformed into a raging torrent that can block the main road to Nizwa. From the main road, only the modern town is visible, but Izki does have a traditional *souk*

Bait Al-Radaidah fort guards the mouth of the wadi

The road up to the Saiq Plateau

(market), and a 150-year-old fort dominates the Sumail Gap.

According to folklore, there is a cave high in the cliffs above the wadi floor where Jarnan, an idol in the shape of a golden calf, was hidden after the new faith of Islam, with its condemnation of idols, became widespread.

103km (64 miles) from Muscat, 26km (16 miles) from Nizwa.

SAIQ PLATEAU

Only reachable by four-wheel drive and with a military pass (your hotel or tour guide can help you obtain this), the Saiq Plateau lies at an altitude of 2,000m (6,562ft). This used to be the rebel heartland. In a handful of villages, there is terracing where vines, peaches, pomegranates, figs and walnuts grow, along with roses from which traditional Omani rose-water is made.

THE JEBEL WAR

By the 1950s, there was much disaffection in Oman about the fact that Sultan Said Bin Taimur (the current Sultan's father), who had ruled since 1932, sat mainly in Salalah in the south, refusing to delegate any decision-making, preferring instead to jealously guard all affairs of state himself. A group of rebel tribal leaders, including one Ghalib who had been elected Imam in 1954, resolved to overthrow the Sultan. At the same time, the Saudis, who had seized Buraimi in 1952, were in full swing in attempting to spread radical Wahhabism throughout Oman. They lent their support to the rebels, who captured several northern towns. The Sultan called on the British to crush the rebels, which they duly did, using mainly air power. Britain was criticised by the UN for intervention in the affairs of another state, and the upshot was an agreement in which Britain paid Oman £250,000 a year. The Sultan's Armed Forces and Air Force were set up to ensure the future security of Oman, with Britain providing seconded officers to help.

Drive: Up the Jebel Akhdar to Jebel Shams

This route takes you to the highest driveable point in Oman, just above 2,000m (6,562ft), and requires a four-wheel drive vehicle for the final stages. The total distance is 37km (23 miles) but a whole day should be allowed to enjoy it fully. Starting just before the town of Hamra, by a petrol station, the dirt track to Jebel Shams is marked on your left.

1 Wadi Ghul

The road was built to enable military vehicles to gain access to the defence installations on the summit. Jebel Shams itself (Mountain of the Sun) is 3,075m (10,089ft), the highest mountain in Oman, and the difference in temperature between the Nizwa plain and the summit can be as much as 30°C. The first 10km (6¼ miles) of the road is tarmac until you reach the village of Ghul, old and new, one on each side of the wadi bed. Abandoned on its rocky outcrop, the old village of Ghul makes a fun exploration for about 45 minutes of clambering around among the eerily empty houses. The name Ghul in Arabic gives us our word 'ghoul', and means a kind of evil spirit that feeds on

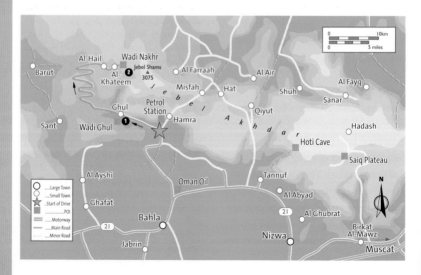

Tannuf lies at the foot of the Jebel Akhdar

dead humans and appears in monstrous shapes.

From Ghul, the ascent up the Jebel begins in earnest on the steep graded track. Allow an hour for this drive, as well as some time to stop and admire the goat-hair rugs woven and sold by the male villagers along the way.

Near the top, Dar Sawda village is signposted 1km (²/₃ mile) off to the left. The main track continues straight up to the restricted military zone, and you must continue and then turn right after 500m (550yds) onto a track signposted Al-Hail. After another 4km (2¹/₂ miles), this will bring you to the plateau. From here, the main track itself ends after 8km (5 miles) at Al-Khateem, a tiny village on the edge of the rim. Before Al-Khateem, many smaller tracks also fork off to the left to the edge.

2 Wadi Nakhr

From this rim, you can look down near-vertical drops of 1,500m (5,000ft) into the truly spectacular Wadi Nakhr below, known as Oman's Grand Canyon. The ground here is scattered with shells and marine fossils, showing it was once the sea bed geological aeons ago.

JEBEL CHILDREN

As you climb up the mountain, tiny villages are signposted off the main track, and are occasionally visible with their hillside terracing. Every day from the age of ten, the children from these villages go to school in Hamra by four-wheel drive. For ages seven, eight and nine, boys and girls are in small village schools learning the basics of reading and writing. You may encounter some of the children up on the plateau, all looking much older than they are because of their heavily weathered skin. They make vital extra cash by selling their little weaving creations, such as key-ring tassels in colourful patterns.

NIZWA

As administrative centre of the interior and Oman's political and cultural capital for many centuries, Nizwa came to be known as the 'Pearl of Islam'. It was favoured by writers, poets, scholars and religious leaders, and today the tradition continues in its fine university. The huge circular fort has come to symbolise the town centre, along with the bright new cobalt blue and gold dome of the Sultan Qaboos mosque that stands beside it.

Falaj system

Nizwa owes its strategic importance to its position on the confluence of two wadis, Wadi Abyadh and Wadi Kalbouh. As you approach from Muscat, you will see the wide wadi bed, usually flowing either weakly or impassably after heavy rains. The town has an extensive network of *falaj* channels (*see p42*) irrigating its date gardens that extend for some 8km (5 miles) behind the town. On the Bahla side of town, look out for the small green sign to Falaj Daris, now set in a garden with a picnic area. Here you can climb down into one of Oman's largest *falaj* channels.

Nizwa fort

Dating back to the 17th century, the powerfully built round tower took over 30 years to complete and is filled in with earth for over half of its 30m (98ft) height and 36m (118ft) diameter.

The mighty round tower of Nizwa fort

The tower created a sound and solid platform for heavy cannon to fire from, and rendered the walls impenetrable by rival cannon. It is entered via a narrow zigzag flight of steps, through a series of three finely carved doors, several centimetres thick, and the deterrent defences are completed with the narrow gap overhead through which boiling water, oil or honey were poured down onto would-be invaders.

The fort within is far bigger than it appears from the outside, and there are seven wells to guarantee the water supply in the event of siege, as well as prisons, storerooms, kitchens, washing areas, sleeping quarters, a mosque, a Koranic school, a *majlis* (reception) room and a judge's room. To the left of the main entrance off the courtyard is a ground-floor exhibition gallery with a fascinating series of pictures explaining the restoration and building techniques, accompanied by 'before and after' photos.

174km (108 miles) from Muscat (2-hour drive); 37km (23 miles) from Bahla (25 minutes' drive). Open: Sat–Wed 9am–4pm, Fri 8–11am. Admission charge.

Nizwa *souk*

Facing the wadi bed is the modern façade of the *souk* (market), and you can drive in here to park. The renovation programme of the 1990s created a sanitised *souk* of unnatural cleanliness for tourists, but just a few steps behind the façade will take you to

Nizwa's traditional renovated *souk*

the pungent backstreets that are a closer representation of the real Nizwa.

The main *souk* area has been imaginatively designed with Omani craft shops selling antiques, silver, jewellery and *khanjars* (traditional Omani curved daggers), pottery, weaving and wooden items. The first shop has a traditional restaurant upstairs with floor cushion seating. Just next door to the left are the refurbished fruit and vegetable *souks*, the fish *souk* and the animal *souk*, at their busiest in the mornings, at weekends and during *Eids* (festivals).

Drive: Fiqain and Manah

Probably Oman's most impressive ruined town, Manah is well worth the short 11km (7-mile) drive south from Nizwa. To reach Manah, take the major fork south towards Salalah that turns off on the eastern outskirts of Nizwa. After just 1km (²/₃ mile), Manah is signposted off to the left, near an outcrop of hills. Some 7km (4¹/₃ miles) after the Salalah turn-off, before reaching Manah, you will notice a picnic spot on a hillock to your left – Seih Al-Barakat.

1 Seih Al-Barakat

Known as Seih Al-Barakat, this is where the Sultan meets the local people after National Day as part of his tour of the whole country meeting people and listening to their grievances.

Take the turn-off marked Fiqain on the right, and follow either of the tarmac roads as they both wind round to meet behind the tall tower. Park near the newly built mosque.

2 Fiqain fort

This remarkable fortified tower house, almost Scottish baronial in its tall, narrow proportions, can be seen from afar rising above the palm trees. It was restored in 1988, and is open approximately 8.30am–2.30pm, or whenever the guardian is present.

The design of the fort is unique, stone built with massive walls and faced with *sarouj* (lime) plaster. There are

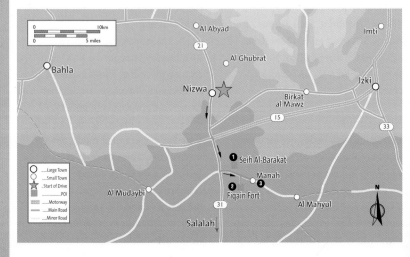

The ruins of Fiqain village

two sets of steep staircases, each leading up to one side of the fort, onto the roof and to fine views over the area. There is a *falaj* irrigation system still flowing nearby, and the fort's well can be accessed from each floor through a specially built hole. The hole was also handy for passing up food on trays or for the family to shout instructions down to the servants. Entry was originally by rope and pulley into the two high windows, and all restoration work in 1988 was carried out using these. The door through which you now enter was a secret entrance, not discovered until 1991. The rooms off the hall were for weaponry, cooking and storage, while the upper levels were used for the guards and soldiers defending the sheikh's family.

All around is the old deserted village, with mud houses crumbling from the rains and through lack of maintenance. A stroll around these makes a fascinating end to the tour, and offers some welcome shade.

At Manah 3km (1³/4 miles) further on, follow the signs to the market, A'Sooq, then turn right at the roundabout by the renovated mosque, following a gravelled track that skirts the stone-built walls of the ruined town.

3 Manah

Currently the subject of a massive restoration project that will take many years, the old town of Manah is called Harrat Al-Bilad. You can still enter the town, and once inside the walls you can find several disused mosques, some with elaborately detailed prayer niches (*mihrabs*). Many of the crumbling houses still have fine carved wooden doors, and a few of the old wells are still in use.

Internal courtyard at Jabrin

BAHLA

From 1150, Bahla was the capital of Oman for four or five centuries under the Nabahina dynasty, a fact that explains the magnificence of the walls that still surround the town for a distance of some 12km (7¹/₂ miles). The walls enclose not only the fort and the town itself, but also an extensive area of date gardens and irrigated fields. Reputedly built some 600 years ago by a woman named Ghaitha, the walls boast a total of 15 gates and 132 towers, some of which can still be viewed. Bahla is also famous for its pottery.

180km (112 miles) from Muscat (2 hours 25 minutes' drive). 200km (124 miles) from Buraimi (2 hours' drive).

Bahla fort

The damage inflicted by enemy attacks or even just severe storms necessitated the rebuilding of Bahla fort many times. One particularly savage attack occurred in 1610, so much of the current fort is almost certainly a Ya'ariba rebuilding, the same as Nizwa, Jabrin, Rustaq and Al-Hazm, though a fort was known to exist here in 1000 BC, making it Oman's oldest fort. Until the 1960s the *wali* used to live in the best-preserved part.

Under continuous restoration since 1993, the fort ranks as a UNESCO World Heritage Site and is considered Oman's most significant monument. The state of disrepair was so advanced when work began that the first two years were spent clearing rubble to return to the original ground level.

JABRIN

A palace rather than a fort, Jabrin is set apart from all other Omani forts through its elegance and elaborate decorations. It was built initially as a home in 1670 and used as a sort of retreat by the Ya'ariba imams; it still retains a calm and peaceful air. The restoration took seven years and was completed in 1983, the first to be undertaken by the Ministry of National Heritage and Culture. The rooms are furnished with antiques to lend an authentic atmosphere.

The fort's location, by itself in a flat, open plain beside some date gardens, shows that it was not designed to have a defensive role. Its builder, the Imam Bil'arub Bin Sultan, had the misfortune to die here in 1692 following a siege by his brother, and his tomb can be seen near the *falaj* (irrigation system), to the left of the main door.

The fort is arranged around two separate courtyards and on three storeys, each with different floor levels, and it boasts a total of 55 rooms. The main reception rooms, known as the Sun Room and the Moon Room because of their astrological motifs, have magnificent painted ceilings. One of the second-floor rooms was known to be allocated to the Imam's favourite horse.

BANANAS FOR THE BRAIN

A famous Koranic school was established on the fort's top floor. Jabrin was a renowned centre for teaching Islamic law, medicine and astrology. An early source records that bananas from the gardens below were fed to the pupils in order to improve their concentration.

12km (7¹/₂ miles) from Nizwa (10 minutes' drive). Allow 90 minutes to see the fort.
Open: Sat–Thur 9am–4pm, Fri 8–11am.
Admission charge.

Bahla fort is being painstakingly restored

Magic, jinn and mysticism

For as long as anyone can remember, Bahla has been known as a centre for magic and sorcery. Stories abound of witches, flying mosques, magic trees and any number of people who are convinced that they have had mystical experiences while in and around the town at night. In Islam, adherents of mysticism were known as Sufis, from the Arabic *souf*, meaning 'wool'. This is a reference to the garment worn by the early ascetic, contemplative and solitary mystics. Sufism strove for a more personal and intense experience of God. Unusually, in Oman many Sufis were women, while in most Muslim countries they were predominantly male.

PROPHET MUHAMMAD'S VIEW

The prophet Muhammad was known to believe in the existence of good and evil jinn, and the Koran has a *Sura* (chapter) called 'Sura of the Jinn'. The word 'genie' came from the Arabic 'jinn', and Muhammad is recorded in the Traditions as saying: 'The Jinn were created of a smokeless fire', just as 'genies' appeared out of nowhere as from Aladdin's lamp. Jinn were said to have a great fear of metal, and someone who thought he was being pursued by jinn would shout 'Hadid, hadid!' ('Iron, iron!'), by way of protection. The existence of jinn in Islam is completely accepted, and through the use of magic, jinn have extended into folklore. A man who died from unnatural causes, for example, was commonly thought to become a jinn spirit and haunt the place of his death as a ghost.

Flying mosques

Just before the town, coming from the Nizwa side, a driveable track leads off to your left and passes through a vast cemetery of simple traditional graves to reach three ruined mosques, set on low hills. You have to climb up to the mosques from the track, and it takes about 40 minutes to explore all three. The nickname of 'flying mosques' comes from the highest mosque – legend has it that it 'flew' here one night from Rustaq. All three are said to have been built for religious hermits. There were several Sufi communities in the area, as at Hamra and even Nizwa. The three mosques are also known as the Mosques of the Saints. Orthodox Islam has no saints, but Sufis saints' tombs are credited with healing powers and are often the object of pilgrimages. The mosques of these three mystics or religious hermits may well be the origin of Bahla's reputation for magic and mysticism.

Flying mosques in the hills behind Bahla

Magic tree

The road opposite Bahla fort leads off into the old *souk* (market) area of town. The shops used to be set around a famous gnarled old tree from which alleyways led off deeper into the *souk*. In one area, animals and vegetables are traded, while in others small silver shops sell old and new jewellery, and in yet others you can buy *khanjars* (traditional Omani curved daggers) and rifles. The tree was reputed to be inhabited by jinn and so the villagers tied it down with chains to stop it being carried off. If you arrive early in the morning, you will see the date auction and the fish market.

HAMRA

Founded in the Ya'ariba dynasty (1624–1741), Hamra boasts Oman's most elegant collection of two- and three-storey mud-brick houses, tucked away in the old part of town. Unusually in this part of the world, it has no fort and no defensive walls, a reflection of the fact that it was never involved in tribal battles, and this explains why the houses are still in such good condition.

Also remarkable is that so many of these old houses are still inhabited, especially those that have easy vehicle access, with air-conditioning and television aerials added. The uninhabited ones are up narrow alleys where no car can penetrate. Some houses still have the town's fast-flowing *falaj* irrigation system running through their entrance hall. One 400-year-old house where a group of female mystics used to live together is known as Bait Al-Safa, House of Purity. Women in the Sufi tradition often formed convent-like groups, devoting their lives to prayer. You can park by the old town gateway and stroll in to follow the *falaj* channel into the heart of the old town. The residents old and young appear friendly and go about their daily business, quite unperturbed by the arrival of foreigners.
40km (25 miles) from Nizwa. Allow 1 hour to explore.

MISFAH

Built into a rock face and now easily accessible on a new 5km (3-mile) tarmac road, Misfah has become a popular destination for trekkers and picnickers; there is even a special shaded picnicking area on the way to the village. At the end of the main alleyway, the *falaj* (irrigation system) ends in pools where the women do the washing and the young boys splash and swim.
5km (3 miles) from Hamra. Allow 1 hour to explore.

Bombed-out ruins of Tannuf from the Jebel War (*see p45*)

The fertile crops round the town of Hamra

TANNUF

The name Tannuf is known for the mineral water that is bottled from the nearby springs. However, the reason to visit is the ruined ghost town, abandoned some 50 years ago after it was bombed by the British Royal Air Force at the request of the current Sultan's father in the Jebel War (*see p45*). The town sits at the mouth of the spectacular Wadi Tannuf, and after parking in the shade by the gorge you can scramble up the collapsing steps to go inside the walls. The Beni Riyam tribe who lived here controlled the Jebel Akhdar (Green Mountain), which is why their sheikhs were called Lords of the Green Mountain. From the wadi behind the town, there were escape routes up into the mountains used by

the rebel leader to slip away to his hideouts in caves high on the Saiq Plateau. Remarkably, the pillared mosque beside the *falaj* irrigation system escaped the bombing and is still quite well preserved, as is the *falaj* itself, running into the gorge where it is built into the sheer mountain wall. After rains, it fills to overflowing and cascades down the wall to join the river. The gorge makes excellent walking, with some pools deep enough for swimming at certain times of year. The magnificent scenery and romantic quiet of the spot encourage lingering, and camping up on the plateau above Tannuf offers wonderful views.

15km (9¹/₃ miles) from Nizwa. Allow 90 minutes to explore.

Tomb remains at Bat, a UNESCO World Heritage Site

BAT AND IBRI

The part of Oman between Jebel Kawr and the border at Buraimi is known as Al-Dhahirah, 'The Back', representing the spine or backbone in Oman's traditional geography, as opposed to Al-Batinah, 'The Stomach', which lies on the other side of the Hajar Mountains. Al-Dhahirah's modern significance lies in its oilfield, notably at Fahud, which produces one-third of Oman's oil.

Bat

Bat is Oman's second UNESCO World Heritage Site after Bahla, and the necropolis here is extensive, with over 100 burial sites, including beehive tombs from the 3rd millennium BC. It covers an area of largely unshaded terrain, so avoid midday visits except in winter.

To the right of the track leading to the necropolis, you will come first to a built circular structure. A Danish team of archaeologists carried out excavations at Bat in the 1970s and dated this complex tower with a well in its centre to 2750 BC. They calculated that it would originally have stood 10m (33ft) tall. They also unearthed human-made water channels leading to the site, the oldest known example of the *falaj* irrigation system in the country.

The main group of Umm Al-Nar tombs lies on the other side of the track from the tower, and attempts have been made to block the track to vehicles. A five-minute walk will take you to the beautifully crafted circular foundations. The tombs were thought to have held about 200 bodies within their 11m (36ft) diameter.

From Ibri, Bat is a 90-minute drive (40km/25 miles). The road is tarmacked to the village of Bat, and, just before the village and a high water tank, fork left onto a dirt track. The fenced ruins lie about 400m (440yds) down this track to the right and left. The tombs are well camouflaged and quite tricky to spot in the landscape of identical-coloured rock. Allow 1 hour to see the site itself.

Ibri

The main town of Al-Dhahirah, Ibri is known for its distinctive black-and-red striped goat-hair rugs, and for its traditional dancing.

The *wilayet* (governorate) of Ibri is the second largest in Oman with around 120 villages, and the modern town of Ibri has a thriving commercial centre, benefiting from its proximity to the Fahud oilfield. The *souk* (market) is well known for its excellent fruit. *297km (185 miles) from Muscat.*

LOCAL DANCES

Traditional songs, dances and poems from the Ibri area are kept alive through regular performances, especially at *Eid* holidays, weddings and births. One dance, Al-Razha, is more like a display of swordsmanship. It is traditionally performed by the local warriors and can signify a declaration of war on neighbouring tribes, announce victory, or mediate between the warring parties. Swords or even rifles are twirled and tossed into the air by rows of men to the accompaniment of drums. The dance can take the form of symbolic duelling and is often performed with verses recited by each tribe alternately. Women are allowed to join in if the event is a wedding or birth celebration.

The fortified town of Sulaif, near Ibri, built in 1138

BURAIMI, WADI FIDDA AND YANQUL

These are the last of the places to visit in Al-Dhahirah region between Bahla and Buraimi. There are no hotels, so camping is your only option, preferably in the superb scenery of Wadi Fidda. A four-wheel drive vehicle is necessary unless you camp on the very edge of the wadi.

Buraimi

Buraimi now joins Abu Dhabi's much bigger city of Al-Ain, and is part of a whole group of villages set in an oasis, mainly belonging to Abu Dhabi with a handful belonging to Muscat and Oman. There is a complex border, with the Omani part named Buraimi and the Abu Dhabi part named Al-Ain, after the largest village in each case. The Saudis tried to lay claim to Buraimi in 1952 on the basis of historical documents and early *zakat* (tax) payments. Their real motive, however, was that they suspected that there were oil reserves in Abu Dhabi territory. The British and the Trucial Oman Scouts drove them out in 1955, but the Saudi presence in Buraimi between 1952 and 1955 was one of the main reasons for the Jebel War of 1957–9 in Oman because the Saudis supported the rebellious Imamate against the Sultan.

Wadi Fidda

The wettest wadi in northern Oman, you are guaranteed water pools here all year round. After rains in the winter,

The fort at Al-Aynain near Wadi Fidda

the wadi may be too wet to drive through, but April and May are perfect, with stunning gorge scenery a welcome diversion from the rather tedious drive from Buraimi down to Nizwa.
From the main Buraimi–Ibri road, follow the signpost to Dank, 14km (8¹/₂ miles). Wadi Fidda is another 24km (15 miles) from the end of the tarmac.

Yanqul

Oman's only gold mine, producing 500kg (1,100lb) of gold a year, opened near Yanqul in 1994. Copper and silver have been found in the surrounding hills, and gold can also be produced from copper oxide deposits. The terrain is certainly unusual, with pointed mountains, some of which are conical, some jagged, some pyramid shaped and some in giant table-top slabs.

The old Yanqul fort and settlement, now deserted, is tucked out of sight 1km (²/₃ mile) beyond a modern government building with flag. Today, it offers a rare chance to explore a fort that has not been restored and a walled village – the residents moved out in the 1970s and into the modern housing provided by the *wilayet* (governorate). The fort still has its heavy wooden doors, and an impressive deep *falaj* (irrigation system) runs within its walls. Inside is a maze of rooms, and on one of the upper floors there is a room with a painted ceiling and Koranic inscriptions on the beams. There is also an unusual mosque that has four domed ceilings and no supporting beams.

HALWA

The sticky sweetmeat offered to all visitors, *halwa* is made in every Omani town, not from grapes as many foreigners fondly imagine, but from gee, semolina and sugar mixed for several hours over the fire with a copper spoon. One early traveller commented that you should on no account watch it being made, 'for feet are usually employed to stir it, and the knowledge of this is apt to spoil the flavour'.

The interior

The Wadi Fidda always has water

The Batinah Coast

This region known as the Batinah, meaning 'innards' or 'belly', runs the length of Oman's coastline from the United Arab Emirates border in the north down to Muscat in the south, a total of some 270km (168 miles). The name refers to the geography of Oman where the Hajar mountains running parallel to the coast are the backbone or spine, and conveys the idea of the 'fat belly' from the wealth of the sea and the fertile date plantations along the coastal plain.

After Muscat and the Capital Area, this is the most heavily populated region of Oman, the villages sprawling along the coast one after another so that they almost merge. The coastal plain is fertile from the mineral-rich soil washed down from the mountains with the rains, and you will notice that the coastal dual carriageway is crossed by many wadis, with their red warning posts marking the depth of the water during flash floods.

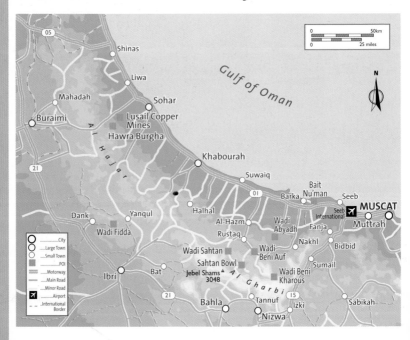

Barka *souk* lies between the beach and the fort

The fishing industry still employs a large proportion of the population here, and fish forms the staple diet of the local people. There are busy fish markets every morning all along the coast – frequently right on the beach, taking the catch straight from the fishing boats. Any excess fish is sold to the towns of the interior.

RACING CAMELS

The Batinah is well known for its breed of camel – the Mussiaha – whose build makes it especially suited for racing. With smaller bodies, bigger heads and a lighter weight than other camels, they are both fast and good at travelling long distances. Camel racing is popular all along the Batinah Coast.

Barka fort by the *souk*

BAIT NU'MAN, BARKA AND SEEB

These places are in the first 60km (37 miles) or so of the Batinah Coast as you head north from Muscat, before the turn-off inland to Rustaq.

Bait Nu'man

This is an unusual fortified country house of particular charm. The restoration of 1990 included full furnishing that helps to convey how it must have been for the family of eight or nine that would have lived here. It was built by the Imam Saif Bin Sultan (died 1711) as his country retreat. *Signposted off the main dual carriageway just south of Sawadi. Open: Sat–Wed 9am–1.30pm. Admission charge.*

Barka

The fine large fort of Barka was restored in 1986. The main road brings you right up to the fort, set on the shoreline by the fish *souk* (market). Fruit and vegetables are also sold here, along with large quantities of animal fodder traded from pick-up trucks.

This is in fact a double fort, the first dating from the Ya'ariba dynasty, the second from the Al Bu Said – this is illustrated by the double gate which has the original Ya'ariba gate on the inside. The decorative carved elements on the doors are very fine, and inside the ground level is raised up to allow good drainage of rainwater or even sea water in particularly heavy storms. All three gun towers can be explored, although the rooms are rather bare.
Reached by forking off 5km (3 miles) towards the sea from the dual carriageway at the same roundabout where Rustaq is marked off inland. Open: 8am–5pm.

THE AL BU SAID DYNASTY BEGINS

The Barka fort in its Ya'ariba incarnation was the setting for the dinner that ended Persian control of the Batinah Coast and heralded the start of the current Al Bu Said dynasty. The *wali* (governor) of Sohar, Ahmad Al Bu Said, formerly a wealthy merchant of wily ways, pretended to reconcile with the Persians by signing a peace treaty. Ostensibly to celebrate, he then invited them to Barka fort for a great banquet, and once they had finished feasting and were flopped on the cushions relaxing, he had them all butchered. The following year, in 1749, Ahmad Al Bu Said proclaimed himself ruler, and proceeded to strengthen the Omani Navy.

Seeb

Known primarily as the site of Oman's only international airport, 40km (25 miles) north of Muscat, Seeb is also Muscat's garden suburb, with many fine weekend villas set among gardens and palm groves. The Royal Stables, the Royal Guard of Oman and the Equestrian Centre are all here, and just off the dual carriageway is the private road to the Sultan's Seeb Palace, Bait Al-Baraka.

NASEEM GARDEN

Omanis are especially fond of parks and gardens, and love the greenery and flowers. At weekends, the parks become very crowded with picnicking families coming for the day. The Naseem Garden is a huge park set between Seeb and Barka. It has an aquarium, lake, waterfall, flower garden, Arabic and Japanese gardens and a train for circuits. *Between Seeb and Barka, signposted off the dual carriageway. Open: Mon–Wed 4–11pm, Thur–Fri 9am–11pm. Tue is for women and children only. Closed: Sat & Sun.*

The Batinah Coast

Bait Nu'man near Sawadi is a fine fortified house

Drive: Sur Rumeis and Sur Majid

The drive along the Batinah Coast can be rather monotonous, so this easy detour makes an interesting and unusual diversion off the coastal dual carriageway. The fortifications also make a good picnic stop.

From Seeb, take the signposted track (fine for a car rather than a four-wheel drive) to Rumeis between Seeb and Barka. The track zigzags between walled date plantations for 1–2km (²⁄₃–1¹⁄₄ miles) until you reach a small town with shops. The road is now tarmacked and you can turn right, parallel to the sea, for a further kilometre (²⁄₃ mile) until you see the towers on the right among the trees. Follow the track around to them.

1 Sur Rumeis

Designed as a place of refuge in times of attack, Sur Rumeis is a fortified walled enclosure (*sur* means 'wall') where village people could congregate. Most *surs* are mud brick, but Sur Rumeis is unique because it was built of

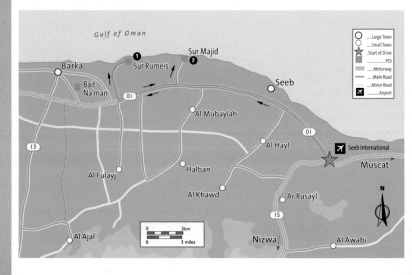

Sur Rumeis coastal fort

stone for extra strength. It even had a moat with a drawbridge. A crumbling mosque with a *mihrab* (prayer niche) stands beside the moat outside the walls. Inside, you can still climb up onto one of the towers.

Between Rumeis and Seeb, a brown sign points to Sur Majid towards the coast and, after 1km (²/₃ mile), the tarmac road leads directly to it.

2 Sur Majid

This *sur* (walled enclosure) is built of traditional mud brick and sits by itself

BULLFIGHTING

On Thursdays and Fridays in the late afternoon, you may happen upon a bullfight along this stretch of the Batinah Coast, the only part of Oman where they are held. The huge humped bulls are pitted against one another in a test of strength, and a panel of judges decides on the winner according to which bull pushes the other to the ground with his horns. No blood is shed and each contest takes only a few minutes.

DATE PALM

There are over 200 different types of Omani date. More than just a tree, the date palm symbolises the rich cultural and historical traditions of the Arab people. Archaeological evidence has shown that dates were used in Egypt and Syria some 8,000 years ago. As a food source, the date is excellent – high in carbohydrates, proteins, vitamins and minerals – but the tree's uses extend far beyond the fruit itself. In Oman, the date used to be called Umm Al-Faqir, meaning 'Mother of the Poor', a reference to the fact that it provided the poor not only with food, but with all the necessary building materials for *barasti* (palm frond) houses and even their furnishings such as beds, woven baskets, mats, sacks and bags. Traditional *shasha* boats were also made from palm trunks and branches. Harvesting begins in early summer.

on the edge of the date plantations. You can walk all around it, but a guard sits by the door and will not let you in because this *sur* requires a permit to visit from the Ministry of National Heritage and Culture (ask your hotel for help).

AL-HAZM AND NAKHL

The inland loop from Barka takes you on a circuit of three of Oman's finest forts, Al-Hazm, Nakhl and Rustaq (*see p72*). Each fort takes at least an hour to visit, and you should allow some time to enjoy the spectacular mountain scenery in the approaches to Jebel Akhdar, where there are many water-filled wadis and picnic spots.

Al-Hazm fort

From the outside, Al-Hazm is probably the most deceptive of all Omani forts. Sitting as it does on the flat, sandy plain some 20km (12¹/₂ miles) from Rustaq,

it appears to lack the grandeur of the better located forts like Rustaq and Nakhl that perch on rocky eminences. Yet the name gives it away – Al-Hazm means 'decisiveness', 'resoluteness' – because the fort makes up what it lacks in natural vantage point in the sheer strength of its defences.

Built in the early 18th century under the Ya'ariba Imam Sultan Bin Saif Bin Sultan, the walls are over 3m (10ft) thick, and were never breached. Inside, there is a veritable maze of rooms linked by secret passageways and tunnels, one of which is said to lead all the way to Rustaq. The fort had its own

The imposing might of Al-Hazm fort

centuries it has expanded from a simple tower into six towers enclosing a series of concentric enclosures that lead through heavily protected gateways, ultimately to the highest and most protected rooms where the ruler and his family lived.

Carefully restored in 1990 using traditional materials, some of these upper rooms have been refurnished in the old style to give an authentic ambience. One room still has a painted ceiling in a fairly simple style.

The preferred layout in all such forts is for the men's living areas to occupy the best position to catch the prevailing wind through their windows, while the women's quarters occupy the hotter inland side. Public meetings are still held once a week in the *majlis* (reception) room. The name Nakhl comes from the Arabic *nakheel* meaning 'date palm'.

120km (75 miles) from Muscat. Open: daily. Free admission.

Nakhl fort with its mountain backdrop

falaj irrigation system, and the restful sound of running water can be heard in many parts of the ground floor.
Open: Sat–Thur 8am–2pm, Fri 8am–noon & 4–6pm. Free admission.

Nakhl fort

This large 350-year-old fort, headquarters of the Ya'ariba in the 18th century, stands proudly on its rocky outcrop, silhouetted against the impressive mountain backdrop. Its massively thick walls follow the natural contours of the rock, and over the

AIN ATH-THOWARAH

These hot springs are a popular picnic spot near Nakhl. At the end of the picnic area is the source of the springs, and there are steps down into the stream that flows all year round. The name Ain Ath-Thowarah means 'Spring of Boiling Water', and while the water is not that hot, it is certainly pleasantly warm and supposedly has medicinal minerals. Local women come here to wash their clothes and dishes.
3km (1³/4 miles) beyond Nakhl, reached by taking the only tarmacked road behind the fort. Then drive on through the date plantations.

Forts

Oman probably has a higher density of forts than anywhere else in the world, a fact that can only reflect how fiercely the warring Omani tribes needed to guard their territory, water supply and oases. In an environment where natural resources were scarce, survival depended on protecting what you had, so virtually every settlement had its watchtowers or fort. Experts have estimated that there are well over 1,000 fortifications scattered around the country, built to defend against neighbouring tribes who might try to seize water or fertile land, and also against foreign invaders. The sheikh of the tribe or the *wali* (governor) would base himself in the fort as his centre of authority, and any rival would have to lay siege to the fort in order to take it, which is why it was so important for each fort to have its own *falaj* irrigation system, preferably fed from

Detail of the fort at Fiqain

Fortified house of Bait Al-Makham in Bawshar

The sheer prevalence and importance of the fort in Oman has had a noticeable influence on the architecture and design of the country's public buildings and private houses, with the national architecture having a distinctive and coherent style. The fort symbolised power and was the centre of the community, so the houses of powerful men copied the characteristics of the fort, where defence was the chief objective. The walls built around these houses have big main gates, and there are crenellations on the tops of the walls. Some even have mock gun slots, and there is a frequent use of towers. Any decorative elements are secondary to the overriding considerations of strength, differing from other Islamic countries where decorative geometric elements are the predominant characteristic.

an unstoppable spring directly below the fort itself.

Apart from the sheer thickness of the walls, the fort was also defended by cannon firing onto the enemy from the towers. In some of the forts, where the twisting passages, staircases and corridors make access to the towers tricky at the best of times, you cannot help wondering how on earth these heavy weapons were ever hauled up to the towers. Cases have been known where cannon have fallen through the roof, their weight too great for the mud ceilings, especially after modern restoration where the *sarouj* plaster used is not made by the old methods and no longer has the same integral strength it had in previous centuries.

THE *WALI* SYSTEM

Oman is divided up into 59 *wilayets* (governorates), each administered by a *wali* (local governor) who is in charge of all civil affairs in his *wilayet*. The *wali* tends to be a prominent local sheikh, appointed by the Sultan. However, he only reports to the Sultan indirectly through the Ministry of the Interior. The system began many centuries ago, but even as recently as the 1980s, if you wanted to visit a fort you had to go first for an audience with the local *wali* and get a 'permission' slip from him – a scribbled note – without which the fort guardian would not permit entry.

The Devil's Tower within Rustaq fort

RUSTAQ

Rustaq, meaning 'Market Town', was
Oman's political and administrative
capital for some 150 years – first as the
Ya'ariba imams' base from 1624, then in
the early part of the Al-Bu Said dynasty
from 1744. It is still an administrative
centre, and the *wilayet* (governorate)
has a population of well over 65,000.
Its location at the exit of a wadi on the
coastal side of the mountains gave it
strategic importance as a commercial
centre for trade between the villages of
the mountainous interior and the
coastal Batinah towns. The mountain
people traded such fruits as grapes,
peaches, pomegranates, figs and
apricots in exchange for fish, lemons
and bananas from the coast.

The town has traditionally been
associated with particular trades,
notably silversmiths famous for
khanjars (traditional Omani curved
daggers) and ornaments, copperwork
and other traditional crafts like making
halwa (a sticky, sweet delicacy). Many
of these skills are being lost today as the
older population dies out and the
young do not want to do manual
labour, but Rustaq is still easily the
largest of the inland towns set on this
side of the Jebel Akhdar.

Rustaq fort

This is Oman's oldest fort, a powerful
structure tucked away at the side of
the wadi bed, renovated in the 1990s.
A tour of the castle, which is furnished
with authentic items wherever possible,
takes at least an hour because the
whole area covers more than 1sq km
(½sq mile). Once inside, there is a

large courtyard area that you can stroll around in a circuit to give you the bucolic feel of the place with its butterflies and wild plants, and the chance to refresh yourself in the old *falaj* irrigation channel. The water still flows strongly and is hot, coming from the nearby hot mineral springs. The congregational courtyard mosque, still in use, used to be renowned for its scholars and as a centre for learning, and its 32 thick pillars can be glimpsed to the right of the fort entrance. The fort itself has four towers, including the mysterious Devil's Tower that has no visible entrance. The finest rooms are at second-storey height and comprise six living rooms, some with painted ceilings in dark red and white geometric patterns. One of the central beams carries Koranic inscriptions listing some of the 99 attributes of Allah, such as the Wise and the Holy. On the ground floor there are prison cells, stores and weapon rooms.

Open: 8am–5pm. Closed: Fri 11.30am–1pm. Admission charge.

Rustaq Souk (Market)

Remnants of the traditional crafts can still be found in the old *souk* opposite the fort. The atmosphere is half coastal, half interior, and it is unusually devoid of Indians. The area is not very big, and it takes about half an hour to browse around. Try to find the traditional sandalmaker, now the last one left, whereas before 1970 he was one of

30 sandalmakers. Omani chests can occasionally be found here, along with *khanjars* and even guns, side by side with herbs and spices, henna, walking canes, tools, water bottles and mousetraps.

The best time to visit is before 11.30am. Fridays are the busiest days.

Doors through to more doors in Rustaq's defence system

WADIS ON THE RUSTAQ LOOP

On the inland circuit between Nakhl and Rustaq, the mountain scenery is spectacular, with many water-filled wadis making fine picnic or camping spots. A four-wheel drive vehicle is necessary to get down into the wadis because the surface is loose gravel and cars will easily get stuck.

Wadi Abyadh

Meaning 'White Wadi' in Arabic, this is famous for its blue pools about 10km (6¹/₄ miles) into the wadi from the main road, and it enjoys lush vegetation.

Surprising pockets of water and vegetation are scattered through the region

Some 10km (6¹/₄ miles) after Nakhl, heading inland, the signpost on the right says 'Al-Mahaleel'.

Wadi Beni Auf

Ten kilometres (6¹/₄ miles) beyond Awabi, a track is signposted to Far, the start of the Wadi Beni Auf, considered by many to be the most visually stunning of any of Oman's mountain drives, ending with the climax of Bilad Sayt, thought to be Oman's most spectacular terraced mountain village. There is talk of a new graded track from Bilad Sayt over the Jebel Akhdar to Misfah, so the drive through the wadi may be extendable in future, although the gradients will always require four-wheel drive. The sides of the gorge are steep, but the ingenious villagers have built terraces wherever possible. Keep left when there is a choice, and after 22km (13¹/₂ miles) you come to the village of Zammah. Bilad Sayt lies 6km (3³/₄ miles) beyond Zammah, up the vertiginous winding track. Tucked away up here, its name is said to be a corruption of the Arabic *bilad nasaytuhu*, meaning 'the town I forgot', because a Moghul general sacked all the villages of the wadi except this one.

Wadi Beni Kharous

The old fort of Awabi sits at the head of a gorge leading into the mountains, and from here there is a track that passes on the left, after about 1.5km (1 mile), a series of 1,500-year-old rock drawings

BEEKEEPERS

Many villages in the Sahtan Bowl are known for their traditional beekeepers. Hives are made from hollowed-out palm-tree trunks and stacked in threes with a small piece of honeycomb inside. The ends are blocked up, leaving just a small gap for the bees to enter. From the time of nesting, the bees take two months to produce the honey, and one hive produces around 100 bottles of honey a year.

on the cliff face and boulders, depicting men and animals fighting. This is the start of the track into the Wadi Beni Kharous, culminating after 30km (19 miles) in the remote village of Al-Mahsanah, where there are ornate castellated houses similar to Yemeni architecture, not found elsewhere in Oman.

Wadi Sahtan

The entrance to the Wadi Sahtan is guarded by the impressive fort of Tabarqah, perched on its cliff edge 9km (5½ miles) behind Rustaq. The narrow ravine continues for some 8km (5 miles), a bumpy drive with strewn boulders and running water at most times of the year, until it enters the impressive Sahtan Bowl, a vast natural plain ringed by mountains. An-Nid is the village here that is often used as the base for an ascent of Jebel Shams, Oman's highest mountain. Donkeys are essential on such an expedition – one donkey per person to carry water, food and bedding for the two days.

The Batinah Coast

Water flows all year round in some wadis in Oman

Wadi-bashing

This graphic expression is expatriate jargon for driving off-road in a four-wheel drive vehicle along a wadi (river bed). The 'bashing' is a pretty accurate description of the damage done by the heavy tyres crushing plant life along the way. While the whole experience is great fun and continually fraught with the excitement and uncertainty of whether you will get stuck, care should be taken wherever possible to minimise the environmental damage done by the vehicle by sticking to previous tracks.

It is only by driving off-road in the wadis of the Jebel Akhdar mountain range that you will truly be able to

Graded track into a wadi

Signs at flash flood points announce the danger for motorists

working jack, a correctly inflated spare tyre, extra fuel, a tyre pressure gauge and lots of water. One person needs 4.5 litres (8 pints) a day in hot conditions. Another useful item to bring along is a piece of old tough carpet that works wonders when placed under a stuck tyre. Tyre pressures are very important; they should be kept high on rocky surfaces to avoid punctures, and low in soft sand to spread the weight of the vehicle.

appreciate the spectacular scenery and realise just how much water there is tucked away in these remote corners. The terrain is very rocky, and geologists call the reddish-brown jagged rocks of the Jebel Akhdar foothills 'ophiolite', rock associated with deep-sea sediments, now pushed above ground. Consequently, a surprising number of sea fossils can be found in the mountains.

It is always best to travel with more than one vehicle so that one can tow the other out. However experienced you are, it is essential to carry a long tow rope at all times, a shovel, a

DRIVING IN WET WADIS

A few simple rules need to be followed in wet wadis to avoid catastrophe. Always cross where the water is at its widest because this tends to be where it is at its shallowest. Never allow the water to go above the tops of the tyres. Always keep your speed down if the water is fairly shallow so that you do not splash the vehicle's electrics. If water is deep, enter slowly in a four-wheel drive vehicle using a low gear (first or second), then keep the revs high once the front grill is in the water to create a slight bow wave.

Do not attempt to start the engine if it does become waterlogged as water may have entered the tops of the pistons through the exhaust or air filter, and this can result in a bent crank shaft, or, worse, a piston breaking through the side of the engine. First tow the vehicle out of the water, remove and dry the spark plugs and dry the ignition system, then turn on the ignition switch which will pump the water out of the combustion chamber. When the water is out, you can reassemble the spark plugs and leads (taking care to get them in the right order), try the ignition or push-start the vehicle if the battery is low.

The imposing white Sohar fort

SOHAR

Considering its historical significance in earlier centuries as the capital of Oman and a major trading port, Sohar today is a shadow of its former self. For over 1,500 years, until 1749 when the Al-Bu Saids moved their headquarters to Muscat, Sohar was Oman's most prestigious and influential town.

The 10th-century Arab geographer Istakhri described Sohar as 'the most populous and wealthy town in Oman and it is not possible to find on the shore of the Persian Sea nor in all the land of Islam, a City more rich in fine buildings and foreign wares than Sohar'. His contemporary, the Arab historian Al-Muqaddasi, described Sohar as 'the hallway to China, the storehouse of the East'. The Portuguese arrived in 1507 to find a thriving town needing 1,000 people simply to defend the fort. They built an Augustine church here, and there had also existed a colony of Jews. The Portuguese retained Sohar until they were driven out in 1650 by the native Ya'ariba sultans.

VANISHED HARBOUR

Difficult even to identify now, Sohar's creek (*khor*) beside the fort is silted up. In its heyday, however, this was a magnificent harbour. Apart from the creek, the other reason for the town's success is its strategic location at the end of the Wadi Jizzi, one of the few east–west passes across the Oman mountain range. Over many centuries, copper was exported to Mesopotamian cities from here.

SINDBAD'S VOYAGE

Sohar was reputedly the birthplace of Sindbad the Sailor, and when Tim Severin set out to recreate Sindbad's voyage to China, the boat he had built from traditional materials to replicate that of Sindbad's was named *The Sohar* on the express wish of Sultan Qaboos. The journey took place in 1981 and lasted a total of seven months, the culmination of three years of planning. The entire project was sponsored by the Sultan as a tribute to Oman's seafaring heritage. Severin hand-picked the timber for the boat from the coast of Malabar in India, where all timber for such ships had come from, because Oman lacked trees large enough to provide first-class boat timber.

Sohar fort

Today, the sprawl of Sohar is still considerable, making it difficult to know when you have arrived at the town centre. Fully restored in 1992, the white-painted fort enjoys a commanding location in front of the beach, opposite the *wali*'s (governor's) office, and it is set in attractively landscaped gardens. The courtyard was excavated in 1980–82 to reveal the brick foundations of a 13th- to 14th-century fort and houses of rich merchants that are attributed to the Princes of Hormuz who had a strong garrison here. Many fine pieces of Chinese porcelain have been discovered. The four-storey keep is now an interesting museum, displaying old weapons, artefacts from the copper trade and navigation equipment, together with a comprehensive historical summary of the area. The fort is said to have a 10km (6¼-mile) escape tunnel.

Open: 9am–1.30pm. Admission charge. Allow 1 hour for your visit.

The lush grounds around the fort

Musandam

Separated from the rest of Oman by a 70km (43-mile) stretch of United Arab Emirates territory, Musandam is Arabia's least known and least populated corner, yet it overlooks one of the world's busiest and most strategic waterways. It covers an area of about 3,000sq km (1,158sq miles), all of which is mountainous, and the coast has fjord-like inlets. Its isolation means that it has only ever been sparsely populated by the semi-nomadic Shihuh tribe and, until the late 1960s and early 1970s, it did not matter much to whom it belonged.

The granting of oil concessions to foreign companies changed all that and allegiance had to be decided and borders formally drawn up. The Shihuh swore loyalty to the Sultan and hence the border was drawn along the edge of Shihuh territory, dividing it off from the tribes whose allegiance lay with the Sheikh of Ras Al-Khaimah. Some of the old tribesmen have since regretted this decision, aware that they might have benefited more from the generous handouts of the United Arab Emirates federal budget.

Speaking a separate language that is a mixture of Arabic and Farsi, the Shihuh have a distinctive culture and lifestyle. It is tempting to speculate that they were the original inhabitants of the region, driven up into the barren mountains by successive waves of Yemeni Arabs arriving from the south. They live in the mountains in the winter rainy season tending to crops and livestock, and migrate down to the coastal settlements in the summer where they harvest dates and fish. Potters and blacksmiths are the main craftspeople. There are thought to be some 200 villages scattered about in the mountains, but only a few are still inhabited, with numbers constantly declining.

Before 1980, there were hardly any roads suitable for vehicles, only precipitous footpaths linking the mountains and the flat, open plains that not even donkeys could negotiate. Many of the coastal towns could only be reached by small boats.

Bare mountains and sea are the characteristic scenery in this region

Fishing is the local mainstay in Musandam

BUKHA

Just 5km (3 miles) beyond the Thibat border entry point into Musandam from Ras Al-Khaimah, Bukha is the first town you will encounter. Its coastal fort, renovated in 1990, sits beside the new road and can be visited when the watchman is on duty. The shallow moat used to fill with sea water before the coastline was pushed further away by the construction of the new road. The fort's most distinctive feature is the round tower on the southwest corner that curves inwards, giving it a pear-shape that had the effect of reducing the impact of cannonballs. The earliest sections have been dated back to the 16th century.

Next to the fort, built up on a raised terrace, stands the Friday Mosque, surrounded on all sides by an extensive cemetery of headstones. A crumbling double set of steps leads down into the ablution area on the inland side. The call to prayer was made from the roof. The once grand mosque is now in a sorry state, most of its roof is missing and much of its delicate stucco plasterwork is flaking off. The only other examples of old congregational mosques such as this are at Rustaq and Bahla (*see pp52 & 72*).

KHASAB

Musandam's largest town, but with a population under 30,000, Khasab acts as the seat of the *wali* (governor), whose influence extends in practice about as far as the limits of the town. Traditionally a community of fishermen, boat-builders, craftspeople and traders, the population surges in summer as people come from Kumzar and the mountain villages to harvest dates and to fish. At low tide, the large shallow bay turns to mud flats, and the type of boat built here was quite flat bottomed but big enough for trading even as far as India. Even today the harbour is busy with small boats bringing such things as goats from Iran, destined for Ras Al-Khaimah, then ferrying back televisions, washing machines and cigarettes to Iran under cover of night when the coast is clear.

Khasab in Arabic means 'fertility', thought to refer to the alluvial silt that has been deposited in the mouth of the large wadi that extends inland for several kilometres. Torrential seasonal flooding has washed the silt down and enabled extensive date gardens to be

ROCK ART

Just 4km (2$^{1}/_{2}$ miles) before Khasab is the oasis of Qida, from which you can follow the signposted track to Tawi. Beyond the village in the centre of a second small village is an enormous cluster of grey boulders, many covered in rock art of ships, horsemen, ibex and camels. Their date and origin remain unknown.

built up. A dam now traps this water, with the bonus that the local diet is supplemented by the duck that are attracted to the pools. The Khasab main fort near the eastern edge of the wadi still survives (*open: 9am–4pm*), an impressive square enclosure with towers at each corner and an old round tower in the courtyard said to be all that remains of the original 17th-century Portuguese fort.

Tour boat in a fjord near Bukha, Musandam

There is never a shortage of boats to rent

BOAT TRIP TO TELEGRAPH ISLAND

From Khasab harbour, the standard boat trip is a one-day outing to Telegraph Island that can be pre-booked or arranged on the spot at the offices opposite the harbour. From October to February, visibility is excellent at about 20–30km ($12^{1}/_{2}$–19 miles). From the end of February, it suddenly drops to about 5km (3 miles), which detracts somewhat from the overall experience. Binoculars should be brought along to help view the excellent bird life along the cliffs and to examine the coastal villages discreetly from afar.

Mooring at Telegraph Island is not always possible because at low tide the boat can damage itself on the rocks. The total tidal variation is just under 1m ($3^{1}/_{3}$ft). Assuming you do manage to land, the island itself is a wonderfully peaceful spot for a picnic, with surprisingly extensive remains of the powerful structures that were built by the British in the mid-19th century.

British interests

The technological revolution in Europe in the mid-19th century and the

DOLPHINS

The boat trip takes you into Khor Ash-Sham, the huge, sheltered inlet where Telegraph Island and a few other islands sit in the calm waters. Here you have a good chance of spotting dolphins as they like the calm water. Attracted by the sound and wake of the boat engine, they enjoy swimming with the boat as if it were a giant dolphin. Once the engine is turned off, they soon lose interest and disappear.

invention of telegraphic communications via a cable transformed the face of worldwide communications. Britain's empire and its links with colonial India had also been revolutionised by the introduction of steamships in 1840. A postal service was started using these ships – first to Calcutta and Rangoon, then to Ceylon and Karachi, extending by 1862 into the Gulf where it linked India with Basra in Iraq.

A telegraphic landline had been laid between Baghdad and Scutari in Albania by 1858, and the next stage was to connect this system to India via a landline to Basra, then a submarine cable down the Gulf. Yet there were difficulties at the Omani end about locating the telegraph terminal on the Musandam tip, and progress was disrupted for a time while the local tribes tried to establish what benefits there might be for them. They regarded the whole affair as a foreign intrusion that had been agreed by the Sultan in Muscat. They had never been consulted, and in any case they did not acknowledge his authority over them. This particular site was chosen as it offered more security than the mainland against potentially hostile tribes, and once the cable was laid and the telegraph station built here, the island was known forever after as Telegraph Island. The station was maintained until 1869, the same year as the opening of the Suez Canal. In practice, though, the terminus only functioned for five years because no one could be induced to live for long in such a remote place.

Typical fjord-like scenery in the calm waters near Telegraph Island

Wildlife

Enthusiastically green in its outlook, Oman is determined to protect its unique flora and fauna, and has several designated nature reserves. Books and studies have been commissioned covering the country's wild flowers, butterflies, birds and other forms of wildlife, making Oman one of the best-documented countries of the Middle East in this field. The Arabian white oryx has been saved from extinction in its special sanctuary on the edge of the Wahhiba Sands (*see pp110–11*). The other creature to merit its own sanctuary is the sea turtle, of which there are three main species – the green turtle, the hawksbill and the loggerhead. It has a designated beach at Ras Al-Hadd (*see pp98–9*). Other reptiles like lizards and snakes are found in abundance in mountain and desert areas, but apart from a few species of viper, most are harmless.

Wild animals found in Musandam, in line with its mountainous and remote geography, are leopards, wolves, foxes, hyenas and the Arabian

Goats enjoy the grazing provided by a lush wadi

Donkeys roam freely and feed themselves

tahr, a sturdy, russet-haired type of mountain goat. On the domestic side, sheep and goats are in paradise here, along with a few donkeys. However, cows, which one could easily imagine happily grazing on the lush plains, do not exist in Musandam and are for unexplained reasons anathema to the Shihuh. Wildlife is abundant in the Rawdah Bowl, with owls, hedgehogs, birds of prey, numerous species of butterfly and amazing cricket life. There are around 80 classified species of butterfly in Oman, mainly in the north and most plentiful in January and February. Their lifespan is a mere three weeks.

February and March are the best months for flowers, and by April the grass is beginning to turn brown.

Oman is on the main migration route for birds heading to southern Africa, with several hundred migratory species. The best times to see these are from April to May and September to October. There are some 80 indigenous species, including eagles and vultures which are best seen in the winter months. Keen bird-watchers with the right timing and location have been able to spot up to 100 species in a single day. Gulls and flamingoes exist in abundance along the coast. The beaches are rich in shells, but Omani conservation laws mean it is forbidden to collect seashells, abalones (type of sea snail) or turtle eggs, just as it is forbidden to drive on sandy beaches. Hunting, collecting or disturbing wild animals and birds is strictly prohibited.

MUSANDAM GEOLOGY

The Royal Geographical Society, which conducted a survey here in 1972–3, concluded that the Musandam peninsula has tilted into the sea by up to 60m (197ft) over the last 10,000 years. In the 1970s, Norwegian adventurer Thor Heyerdahl sailed his replica Sumerian boat *Tigris* down through the Gulf towards the Straits of Hormuz, and wrote memorably of his first sight of Musandam: 'above the cloud banks, raised above the earth was land, like another indistinct world of its own. Solid rock was sailing up there … with rock walls dropping almost perpendicularly into the sea.' (*The Tigris Expedition: In Search of our Beginnings*, 1980)

THE SAYH PLATEAU AND RAWDAH BOWL

Heading inland past the Khasab Motel and beyond the little airport into Wadi Khasab, you come to a major junction with large signposts. To the left is the way to the beach of Khor Najd and the forested plain

Lush vegetation of the Rawdah Bowl

of Sal Al-A'la, both potential camping spots within 30 minutes of Khasab, while straight on leads to the spectacular military road up and over Jebel Harim, Musandam's highest peak at 2,087m (6,847ft), and down the other side to the checkpoint at Wadi Bih. Only Omani passport holders are permitted to pass through this checkpoint.

Ascent to Jebel Harim

Low-ratio four-wheel drive is required for this ascent, probably the most difficult stretch of driving in Oman – more difficult than the drive up to Jebel Shams or up to the Saiq Plateau, both of which have wider routes with better compacted surfaces. You also need more of a head for heights here because some stretches are extremely vertiginous. The scenery throughout is stunning. Towards the upper part of the ascent you suddenly arrive at the Sayh Plateau, an attractive miniature plateau 2km (1¼ miles) long and 0.75km (½ mile) wide. Donkeys, sheep and goats frolic in the surprisingly lush pasture land.

Rawdah Bowl

Descending the mountain of Jebel Harim, you come to a crossroads. If you go straight over, it leads you into the Rawdah Bowl, the best camping spot in the area. The five-minute drive along a good track heads through a narrow defile then abruptly opens up into a large mountain-ringed

BAIT AL-QUFL HOUSES

Just beyond the spectacular summit pass, look to the left for a small settlement of stone houses that can be reached by a small fork off the main track. Here you have a rare chance to explore these characteristic Musandam mountain houses. The design is geared around security, and the name Bait Al-Qufl (House of the Lock) refers to the highly complex locking device that was used to ensure no one could enter the house during the summer months when it was left unattended while the villagers went down to the coast. There are no windows and the few possessions were locked inside – storage jars, cooking utensils and tools. Around the village are complex walled field systems, the walls carefully placed to follow the natural contours of the ground for optimum rainwater collection. This part of Oman has no *falaj* irrigation system (*see p42*) as there would never be enough water to keep them running.

bowl, some 5km (3 miles) long by 2km (1¼ miles) wide. There are a few settlements in the bowl and two interesting cemeteries with tall headstones, but the area is large enough to find corners tucked away, often close to ruined stone houses. These cemeteries are a Sunni, Hanbali style, a complete contrast to the small discreet stones of the typical Ibadhi graveyard. In the plain near the entrance to the Rawdah Bowl is a grouping of some 15 cairn tombs, as yet undated and unexcavated, but certainly unique in Musandam. One tomb has a long, narrow chamber in the centre with roof slabs over the top.

Eastern Province (Sharqiyah)

Known as the Sharqiyah (sharq means 'east'), Oman's Eastern Province is separated from the Jebel Akhdar interior by the Sumail Gap. For years, the Sharqiyah has been, and still is, dominated by the Al-Harithy tribe and its sheikhs who are fervently Ibadhi (see pp96–7). The landscape here is gentler than the harsh colossal massif of the Jebel Akhdar, with a mix of softer mountains and plains that appear almost African at times.

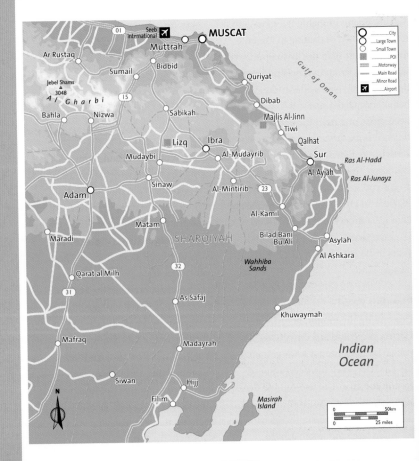

The African links go further than appearance. After the Zanzibar revolution of 1963, large numbers of Omanis fled East Africa and sought asylum in Oman, the country that many considered to be their homeland due to the trade links that went back to the 17th and 18th centuries, favouring the Sharqiyah because of ties with the Al-Harithy tribe. African goods used to be imported to Oman via the ports of Sur and Al-Ashkara, and dates were exported in exchange.

It takes about one hour's drive from Muscat to reach the fork south into the Sharqiyah, just beyond Bidbid on the main Nizwa road. At this point, Sur, the chief town and harbour of the Sharqiyah, is signposted as 263km (163 miles), a drive of about three hours on good tarmac roads. There is no more dual carriageway, but the

CAVING

In 1983, an American geologist working for the Ministry of Water Resources stumbled upon the second-largest cave chamber in the world at 310m (1,107ft) long and 225m (738ft) wide. Known locally as Majlis Al-Jinn, the cave's correct title is in fact Khosilat Maqandeli. Reached by a two-hour trek from the nearest village of Karan, it then involves a 160m (525ft) rope descent through a sinkhole to reach the floor of the cave – clearly an enterprise that should not be undertaken lightly.

roads are fairly empty. The initial stretch leads you through attractive scenery, winding through wadis and gorges with low hills all around, and there is quite a lot of water in the wadi crossings after rain. After about 60km (37 miles), the road leaves the hills and wadis behind and crosses flat, open terrain.

Eastern Province (Sharqiyah)

The huge expanse of beach at Sur

The shipyards at Sur are in decline

SUR

The name Sur is exactly the same as that of the coastal port of Sur in Lebanon, known to Westerners as Tyre. One interesting theory, based on Herodotus' account that the Phoenicians came from the Gulf area, is that the Phoenicians originally came from Oman, then moved on to Lebanon, reusing the name of their home town. There is no archaeological evidence to support this theory, but certainly the rocky spit by Sur creek does resemble that of Tyre, and the origins of the seafaring Phoenicians remain unclear and controversial.

Long famous for dhow building, Sur continues to be the largest centre for what remains of the industry in Oman. In the 19th century, some eight dhows a year were built and launched, whereas now it is only one or two. The workers are invariably Indian.

If you follow the main tarmac road into the centre of town, this eventually brings you to the seafront and continues in a big loop around the lagoon, on the edge of which are the boatyards, still in operation and easily visited. You can wander in through any of the gates in the boatyard. The keel and hull of the boats are constructed of huge imported Indian teak logs, while smaller pieces of local acacia wood are used for the ribs. The Arab building technique does not have the limitation of plans: the boats are always built by eye, from the outside in, ribs first, rather than using the Western convention of inside to out.

Beyond the boatyards, the road winds in a loop past a restored 80-year-old dhow. One of the last ocean-going vessels to be built in Sur, it is 20m (66ft) long and weighs over 300 tons. Discovered in Yemen, the boat was brought back by a local retired captain after money was

SLAVE TRADE

As recently as the early 1960s, some 3,000 residents of Sur had worked overseas in India, East Africa and the rest of the Arabian Gulf, a rare thing given the inward-looking character of the interior. Slave trading and arms trafficking were their main preoccupations, a form of trade they regarded as totally acceptable then. When the British intervened to eradicate this trade in 1822, their well-meaning attempts to stop it were viewed with puzzled incomprehension. In order to escape British attempts to control their shipping, the Sur merchants simply used the French flag, a practice actively encouraged by the French in the late 1800s.

raised from Sur inhabitants to display it as a symbol of the town's maritime heritage. At low tide, the other dhows are beached on a grubby and unsightly expanse of wet mud.

Al-Ayjah

Sur today has almost no elegant 18th-century merchant houses, and you will need to visit Al-Ayjah across the lagoon by the lighthouse to see some. Before the new tarmac road was built, skirting the 10km (6¼ miles) around the lagoon past the mangrove swamps, the town was only reached by ferry, and the inhabitants relished their independence, setting up their own customs post and flag.

Al-Ayjah lighthouse across the bay from Sur

A *sabla* in Al-Mudayrib

AL-MUDAYRIB

Beyond Ibra on the road to Sur, this small town is worth an hour's visit, especially towards the end of the day when the distant Wahhiba Sands glow gently in the sunset. Follow the road into the centre of Al-Mudayrib, towards the watchtowers, to arrive at the picturesque town square, and then take the time to wander among the fine old buildings. Ten of these, known as *sablas*, are still used as public reception areas for meetings, weddings or halls of mourning after a death.

IBRA

On the main Sharqiyah road from Bidbid to Sur, Ibra is the largest inland town, sprawling over a large area with several wadis. Ibra is the home of the Al-Harithy tribe, Ibadhi Muslims of aristocratic descent who have featured large in the country's history. The town used to have close trading links with Zanzibar and East Africa, and this prosperity, less evident today, was very apparent in old Ibra, where the houses of wealthy merchants still stand crumbling among the palm gardens.

Ibra has two old quarters, and they are both reached by forking to the right where the signpost says Ibra Sufelat (Lower Ibra). After 1.5km (1 mile), turn right towards Kanaatir, following the track down into the stony wadi bed, accessible by car. Almost immediately you will come to two ruined grand houses on the right-hand side. Some 400m (1,300ft) further on, look out to your left for a fine gateway set in the edge of the palm plantations lining the wadi, the entrance to the old quarter of

Kanaatir. A few houses at the edge are inhabited, but further into the middle the entire area is deserted. There is an evocative derelict *souk* (market) in a pillared courtyard on the right.

Fork left at the far end of the village and walk along the winding track through the lush plantations for 10 to 15 minutes to arrive at Al-Minzfah, the old quarter of Ibra where Oman's grandest merchant houses are to be found. Entering the quarter through an impressive gateway, you cannot miss the fine houses that are built of stone faced with mud plaster, some of them four storeys high. Their state of repair is variable, one or two are locked and impregnable, while others no longer

WOMEN-ONLY *SOUK*

Unique in Oman, Ibra's modern quarter boasts a Women-Only *Souk* (Market) and men are forbidden to enter. Shopping was traditionally seen as the man's role, so that the wife could be kept safely at home away from prying eyes, but here the women do the selling as well as the buying, concentrating on women's items like perfumes, cosmetics and clothing, as well as fruit and vegetables. 'Men do not enjoy shopping like we do', says Fatima, a regular visitor, 'We like to take our time and chat while buying, but they want to get it over with.'

Women-Only Souk. *Open: Wed 7.30–11am.*

have doors and can be wandered around at will. A few concrete modern houses have now been built among them, spoiling the magnificence of the ruins.

The wadi leading to old Ibra passes some fine old merchants' houses

Ibadhism

Ibadhism is an early sect of Islam that exists today only in Oman and in small pockets of North Africa and Zanzibar, having been wiped out in all other parts of Arabia. Ibadhi are deeply conservative and traditional, their beliefs based on the earliest Islamic sources, the Koran and the Hadith (Sayings of the Prophet Muhammad). The sect is known for its simplicity and moderation. It believes the Imam (spiritual leader) must be elected by the whole community, and if he loses support or credibility he may be removed or deposed. If no suitable Imam can be found, the office can remain unfilled until such time as the community agrees on a worthy candidate. There was, for instance, a gap of 60 years from 1810 to 1870. At one stage, three candidates in a row refused the position after being elected.

Special attention is also given to *difa*, the defence of territory and religion. The Imamate had always tended to be inward-looking, detached from the activities of the coast. This isolation has given them a strong sense of community that has permitted Ibadhism to endure here. Named after Abdullah Ibn Ibadhi (c.AD 683), the Ibadhis were the most tolerant sub-division of the puritanical Kharijites who bitterly opposed both Ali, the fourth caliph, and the right of the powerful Meccan Quraysh tribe to choose the caliph. The Ibadhis wanted the Islamic state to return to how it had been in the time of the Prophet, before the power struggle between Ali and Mu'awiya (the Sunni/Shi'a split), and believed that the best person for caliph should be chosen regardless of his relationship with the Prophet's family. This disagreement

Ibadhi mosque in the village of Fiqain

Simple village mosque in the interior of Oman

ended in persecution and exile for the Ibadhis in the late 7th and early 8th centuries. Some took refuge in Oman and others in Zanzibar, Libya, Tunisia and Algeria, where they still survive.

Ibadhis differ from Sunnis and Shi'a (the two main Islamic sub-divisions), in that they do not feel it is essential for a visible leader to exist at all times. Imams were appointed from the 8th century onwards in Oman as spiritual, political and military leaders. Sometimes known as 'quietists', Ibadhis believed in achieving things through quiet dignity and reasonableness, not through fanaticism. Their mosques reflect this approach and tend to be quite austere, with just the minimum of decoration around the *mihrab* (prayer niche) and windows. Even minarets

were not used except on the coast, and in the interior the call to prayers was simply made from the roof, reached by an outside flight of steps.

Christians and Jews have always been tolerated by Ibadhis, and they have been permitted to practise their own religions in Oman. In spite of this, Christians were frequently served last in the coffee-pouring etiquette where guests were always served in order of importance.

In keeping with their puritanical ethic, Ibadhis usually regard singing and dancing as a frivolity. The strongly Ibadhi areas are the whole of the Sharqiyah, Bahla to Izki, and the Jebel Akhdar, which provided the refuge for Ibadhism and the Imamate during periods of outside intervention and dominance.

Drive: Ras Al-Hadd and Ras Al-Junayz

This excursion to watch turtles hatching on the beaches at Ras Al-Hadd and Ras Al-Junayz involves an overnight stay because you have to be up at dawn to catch the moment. You can either camp or stay in the hotel accommodation nearby.

The drive from Muscat to Ras Al-Hadd via Bidbid and Sur takes a total of 6 hours and is a distance of 323km (201 miles). The final stretch from Sur and Al-Ayjah is a 2-hour drive along graded track. It is clearly signposted.

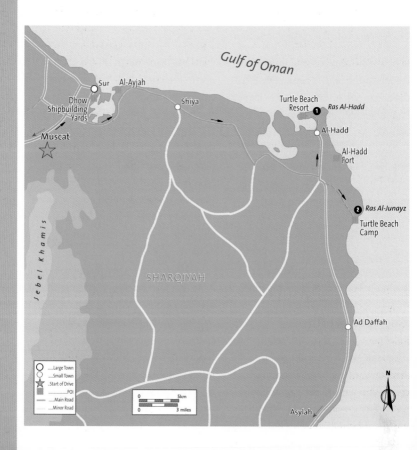

1 Ras Al-Hadd

To the north of the easternmost cape of Oman, Ras Al-Hadd is the headland where the turbulent Indian Ocean meets the calmer Gulf of Oman – a flat sandy spit at the end of a monotonous plain. The remains can still be seen of the airstrip of a British Royal Air Force staging post built here in World War II. A collection of *barasti* (palm frond) huts nearby was where simple fishermen lived, with a fort set above them. The white-painted fort (*open: Sun–Thur 8am–2pm*) is worth visiting for the views from the towers.

An estimated 20,000 turtles use the beaches of Ras Al-Hadd and Ras Al-Junayz as nesting grounds each year. They can be seen hatching all year round, but the biggest numbers are seen between June and September. The turtles migrate from as far afield as the Red Sea and the East African coast. *The next settlement along the coast is Ras Al-Junayz, 10km (6¼ miles) southeast of Ras Al-Hadd – it is clearly signposted.*

2 Ras Al-Junayz

The government has established a Turtle Beach Nature Reserve here, along with a campsite that provides simple *barasti* (palm frond) huts, water and toilet blocks. The guides who staff the reserve will escort you to the beach at dusk to watch the large female turtles come ashore to lay their eggs. Then, just before dawn, you are allowed unescorted onto the beach to watch the

Turtles need quiet, sandy beaches to lay their eggs safely

eggs hatching and the baby turtles running the gauntlet to reach the sea before the waiting gulls or crabs can devour them. Many do not survive this first test. The wardens have to keep records of the numbers nesting each night, but no records are kept of the hatching process. Torches or flash photography are not permitted.

TURTLES

Around 20,000 green turtles nest along 1,700km (1,056 miles) of the coast of Oman, the largest nesting population in the Indian Ocean. Masirah Island has the world's largest nesting population of loggerhead turtles – 30,000 from April to July alone – and they are thought to lay around 3 million eggs a year.

The hawksbill, the most endangered of all turtles, nests on the Damaniyat Islands in the largest numbers, and on other beaches throughout Oman in smaller numbers. As few as two or three in every 10,000 are estimated to survive until adulthood. Those that make it to the sea without being eaten by birds, cats, dogs, foxes or crabs then face the perils of fishing nets, as well as direct hunting by humans and other predators.

View into the Wadi Shaab gorge

DIBAB, QALHAT, TIWI AND WADI SHAAB AND WADI DAYQAH

The coastal road between Sur and Muscat is the most scenic route through the Sharqiyah. At the time of writing it still requires four-wheel drive for the stretch between Tiwi and Dibab, although that may change in future.

Dibab

The beaches in this area are well worth exploring, with unusual shells and plentiful bird life. Also at Dibab, about 5km (3 miles) beyond the village, is a huge natural sinkhole – 40m (131ft) across and 20m (66ft) deep – known locally as Bait Al-Afreet (House of the Demon). The water inside is clear, green and slightly salty, and you can swim here. You can even snorkel to see the colourful sponge life.

Qalhat

Now accessible by graded track either from Sur (20km/12^1/2 miles) or from Tiwi to the north, Qalhat used to be an hour's drive by Land Rover from Sur. In the 15th and 16th centuries, the city was in its heyday, an important port with a *falaj* irrigation system leading down the wadi from the hills, with many wells to supplement it. An earthquake put an end to the town's prosperity, and it never recovered.

The site today is remarkably extensive, and warrants a stop of at least 90 minutes, for which you will be rewarded by the discovery of much interesting pottery, arched cisterns from the 13th century built by the Princes of Hormuz, and a fecund plant and butterfly life. The small harbour can be reached by a 20-minute stroll from the road. Most visitors make a brief stop to look at Bait Maryam, the House of

MARCO POLO

The famous traveller wrote of Qalhat:
The city has a very good port, much frequented by merchant ships from India and they find a ready market here for their wares, since it is a centre from which spices and other goods are carried to various inland cities and towns. Many fine war horses are exported from here to India, to the great gain of the merchants.
The Travels, Penguin Classics, 1958.

Mary, the only major building to survive, originally said to have been covered in glazed tiles.

Tiwi and Wadi Shaab

Both of these settlements are located at the mouth of gorges that share their name. Wadi Shaab is one of the most scenically beautiful wadis in all Oman, accessible only on foot by a small bridge that leads into it. You will pass steep ravines, pools, waterfalls and lush plantations, culminating in a deep mountain pool at the end of the wadi. At Tiwi, the gorge is wider and still driveable for the first 10km (6¹/₄ miles).

Dayqah

Meaning 'Narrow Wadi', Wadi Dayqah is one of Oman's most famous wadis, an old pack-animal route from the coast to the interior and still used until the 1980s. At 14km (8¹/₂ miles) in length, it is the longest perennially flowing wadi in Oman, with many deep pools. The head of the wadi is called the Devil's Gap, where the walls are 1,700m (5,578ft) high and the gorge narrows to 12m (39ft) – one of Oman's best canyon excursions to be done on foot.

Bridge across Wadi Shaab

Bedouin lifestyle

Until the 1960s, the Bedouin in the south of Oman lived a lifestyle of austerity that is difficult to imagine. As nomads, they owned nothing but their camels, goats and a few leather bags (the Arabic word *bedu* means 'desert-dweller', and the plural used in the West is 'bedouin'). Against the odds, the Bedouin sustained themselves, even managing to have children who often slept squashed among the goats. This intimate reliance on nature, where they could die if a well dried up or a camel died,

Camels adore the leaves of the acacia tree

gave them a deep sense of dependence on the will of Allah.

Despite the Bedouin's extreme poverty, the rule of hospitality in the desert was to share with guests and unexpected visitors, even at the expense of your own family. It was not acceptable for a Bedu to eat or drink until his companions had all reached the well, and no one would take more than his share. Petty theft within the tribe was despised as dishonourable. However, in the interests of survival it was acceptable, even manly, to raid another tribe's camels, and to kill their tribespeople in order to steal for your own. Blood feuds were not crimes but a question of honour and would last for generations. The Arab proverb runs: 'After 40 years the Bedu took revenge and said: I have been quick about it.'

The camel

Perfectly adapted to the harsh desert environment, the camel is the lifeblood of the Bedouin. It does not sweat until its body temperature exceeds 40°C (104°F), which enables it to conserve its water for long periods even in excessive heat. If there was no water, the Bedouin relied on the camel's milk. To ensure the camel population did not decline, a Bedu who owned she-camels would arrange a meeting with a he-camel belonging to another Bedu and borrow its services in exchange for milk or food. From the footprint of a camel, any Bedu could tell who its owner was, and from the texture of its droppings he would know when and where it had last drunk, and in which wadis it had eaten.

With changing lifestyles and increasing sedentariness, fewer people wish to own camels these days because they are not profitable and the status that used to go with owning a large herd is fast evaporating. The cost of a camel for meat is around RO120, a price that goes down annually as fewer and fewer people can be bothered to look after the camels and pay for the expensive fodder in the months beyond the monsoon period. A camel providing milk sells for around RO500, but a racing camel can sell for a great deal more, even over RO1,000. Consequently and not surprisingly, the Bedouin of Oman are dying out because their lifestyle is no longer viable in the 21st century.

CRIME AND PUNISHMENT

Crime is practically unknown in the Hadramaut; such things as robbery and murder, being done according to established rules, come rather under the heading of legitimate warfare.
Freya Stark, *The Southern Gates of Arabia*

WAHHIBA SANDS

Oman's mini-version of the Ar-Rub' Al-Khaali (the Empty Quarter), the Wahhiba Sands are a desert of shifting dunes covering 180km (112 miles) from north to south, and 80km (50 miles) from east to west. The most impressive dunes, some rising to 100m (330ft), can be found along the northern end of the Wahhiba, getting ever lower the closer you are to the coast in the south. Since the dunes flow in corridors north to south, orientation is relatively simple as long as you always drive in straight lines. However, an east–west crossing is tricky, virtually guaranteeing many hours spent getting lost and digging out your vehicle (*see pp76–7*).

One of the best entrances to the Wahhiba Sands from the north is by the Al-Mintirib/Bidiyah fort. If you intend a full crossing, make sure you have a full tank from the petrol station on the main road. The exit points in the south are anywhere on the road between Hayy and Al-Nuqdah, and the total distance north–south is the full 180km (112-mile) length of the sands.

If you are in a single vehicle but want to experience the sensation of desert without danger, you do not need to venture into the sands proper. An alternative option is to drive from Al-Mintirib/Bidiyah fort 7km (4^1/3 miles) east (left) to Al-Huwayah, a large oasis on the very edge of the Wahhiba with extensive date and banana plantations. Here, the high dunes completely encircle the oasis. You can camp just beyond the plantation on the edge of the desert, or you can simply picnic in the shade with a view of the spectacular dunes pressing in. From June to September, at the height of summer, the few remaining Wahhiba Bedouin families come to the oasis complete with livestock. They live in the *barasti* (palm frond) huts on the edge of the town to harvest their dates. A gravel road from here heads 24km (15 miles) into the desert before becoming a sand track; you can venture a little way along it if you dare.

In 1986, the Royal Geographical Society conducted an expedition to the Wahhiba, and their findings aroused international scientific interest. There were 35 scientists on the team, and they discovered 150 species of plant, 200 species of mammal, birds, reptiles and amphibians, and 16,000 invertebrates.

A curious phenomenon can be found along the eastern edge of the Wahhiba in the form of an area of extensive woodland of Prosopis (*ghaf*) and acacia living entirely on dew, with scattered Bedouin shanty towns among them.

UNIQUE DESERT

No body of sand in the world contains such a full range of study terrains, nor has so much to offer desert scientists urgently trying to piece together the complex jigsaw of arid zone areas. Its isolation and size lend itself to field research simply because it can be studied as a complete unit. It can be circumnavigated by Land Rover in three days.

Project Director, Royal Geographical Society, 1986

Encroaching sands of the Wahhiba Desert

Dhofar

Lying in the extreme south of Oman, Dhofar borders Yemen to the southwest and Saudi Arabia to the northwest. In many ways, it is like a separate country within Oman – different tribally, culturally, economically and even climatically. Nevertheless, politically Dhofar has belonged to Muscat since 1879. Sultan Qaboos' father, Said Bin Taimur, always preferred it to Muscat, often choosing to live in Dhofar, and for the last ten years of his life he did not leave it at all.

Hundreds of years of shared interest in the frankincense trade routes have meant that the Dhofari people are closer to the Hadramaut tribes of Yemen than to the northern Omanis. Originally, the Dhofari were said to be a mountain tribe arriving with the Queen of Sheba when she took control of the hillsides of frankincense trees. Today, they still speak four dialects – Mahra, Shahra, Kharous Harusi and Botahari – linguistically different to

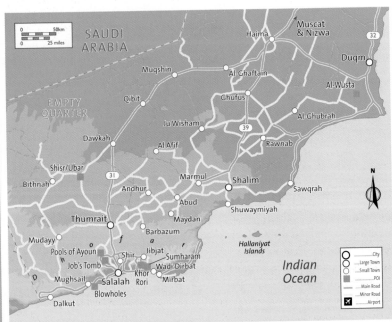

Dhofar's climate encourages exotic flowers

Arabic. Estimates of the numbers of Dhofari range between 10,000 and 15,000. Sultan Qaboos is himself half-Dhofari (his mother was from Dirbat) and he grew up in Salalah. After returning from his army training in Sandhurst in the UK, he was kept there under virtual house arrest by his father.

The Dhofari mountains and the Salalah plain together catch the edge of Africa's monsoon climate, with daily rains from mid-June to mid-September. Over 38cm (15in) of rain falls in these months, turning the wadi beds into deep rivers and making dramatic waterfalls gush over steep cliffs. All visitors are amazed by the luxuriant greenery that follows the rains, at its best from mid-September to late October, and this is the ideal time to visit, when daytime temperatures average 28°C (81°F).

A cargo ship in the busy port of Salalah

SALALAH

More like a town set among coconut plantations, Salalah is the capital of Dhofar province and is regarded as Oman's second city despite its population of a mere 150,000. The name itself means 'Shining One' in the Jebali language.

The drive down from northern Oman is over 1,000km (620 miles) of excruciatingly dull landscapes and is not to be recommended. Most visitors, therefore, arrive by air, with fine views on landing of the Qara mountains and the fertile Salalah plain by the sea. The tiny airport is just 2km (1¼ miles) north of the town centre, and only one plane is ever processed at a time so you are off into your taxi within minutes of touchdown. The route to the beach hotels winds through lush plantations of coconut, papaya, banana and mango, giving the place an African feel. There is almost no high-rise development, just single and double storey, and any industrial development is tucked away in a totally separate zone to the west of town around the port.

The best time for a visit is October to February when Westerners can escape the winters of their own countries in exchange for some tropical heat and sunshine with temperatures around 25–30°C (75–85°F). The greenest time is September, and by late October all traces of the post-monsoon greenery have disappeared.

Al-Balid archaeological site

Set on Khor Salalah (Salalah Creek) and covering an area 2km (1¹/₄ miles) long and 0.6km (¹/₃ mile) wide, this is the site of ancient Salalah, known as Zufar, from which the province of Dhofar gets its name. Dating from the 10th–15th centuries, the city traded in incense and Arab horses, gradually declining in the 16th century when the Portuguese dominated the exported trade to India. Some of the ruins are quite powerfully built and include the ruler's palace, a Great Mosque, a Koran school and the cemetery. There are also signs of a large enclosing wall with towers. German archaeologists have been responsible for excavating the site, and they are optimistic that radiocarbon dating will prove that an older settlement dating back to Roman times is under the medieval one. They are sure Zufar would have been settled as a port exporting frankincense at this time.

Souks (Markets)

Half a day is all you will need for a tour of Salalah. In the centre there is the old souk (market) where frankincense and gold and silver jewellery can still be bought. Located close to the Sultan's palace/fort, Al-Husn, the souk area is known as Al-Hafa, a sprawling maze of little alleys where the small number of Salalah's remaining old houses are to be found, now inhabited by Pakistanis and Bangladeshis. The Omanis prefer the modern suburbs these days. A handful of shops still sell old silver jewellery like Omani *khanjars* (traditional Omani curved daggers), women's anklets, bracelets and headdresses, but each year there are fewer and fewer. Colourfully dressed Dhofari women are often to be seen in the *souks*, sometimes even as the stallholders, bargaining like the men and always unveiled.

The best times to visit the souks *are 8–11am & 4–7pm. They are closed on Fridays.*

Coconut palms are a common sight on Salalah's beaches

Dhofar

Reintroduction of the oryx

Oman has possibly the most enlightened policy on conservation in the Middle East. Sultan Qaboos is deeply aware of the importance of preserving not just nature and the environment, but also the national architecture, crafts, traditions, music, dance and wildlife.

The Arabian white oryx was virtually extinct in the 1960s, but through a captive breeding programme with donated animals from London Zoo, Kuwait and Saudi Arabia, oryx were successfully reintroduced in the early 1980s in the Arabian Oryx Sanctuary near Al-Kamil on the edge of the Wahhiba Sands.

In 2007 the reserve lost its status as a World Natural Heritage Site when it was opened to oil prospectors. In the Wadi Yalouni in 1972, the last herd of wild oryx in Oman were hunted to extinction by a hunting party from abroad. Sultan Qaboos decided that the oryx should be reinstated on the same spot and protected by the Harasis tribesmen of the Jiddat, as the region is known.

In 1976, the Sultan ordered that all possible means should be pursued to bring these animals back, and in March 1980, after years of planning,

Oryx leucoryx in the Jiddat sanctuary

JIDDAT AL-HARASIS

Between Nizwa and Salalah, much of the Omani desert is not rolling sands at all, but flat gravel plain, black or occasionally purplish-green in colour. The stretch northeast of Salalah is known as the Jiddat Al-Harasis, and the Harasis tribesmen are considered the purest nomads in Oman. They own no date plantations, but migrate with their camels in search of grazing on the inhospitable lowland Jiddat, and they speak a South Arabian dialect incomprehensible to any other Arab. The Jiddat landscape can turn green after heavy rains, with lakes that can linger for months in the desert, extending 2km (1¼ miles) long by 1km (⅔ mile) wide, deep enough to swim in. Creatures whose eggs have lain dormant for up to ten years then hatch out, newt-like, and live in the lakes.

Gravelly desert of the Jiddat Al-Harasis

five oryx from the World Herd of Arabian Oryx in the USA were sent over, kept in enclosures, and eventually joined by nine more. By 1982, the first herd of some 40 Arabian oryx was released into the wild, and by 1996 the number exceeded 270, 95 per cent of which were born in the desert. Rangers were recruited from the local Harasis tribe, of whom every man, woman and child has pledged to protect the oryx.

Like camels, oryx are supremely well adapted to a desert environment, conserving their water intake and only requiring a drink every few months – the actual record is 22 months! They achieve this by grazing on various plants that have a high water content. Their life span is around 19 years, and their white coat reflects the sunlight and serves as camouflage.

CAMPING

If you camp anywhere on the Jiddat, the kind of wildlife you encounter in the evening is the fennec fox with its gigantic ears, jerboa, desert hares and lizards. The Harasis regard the fennec fox as a kind of mascot; they leave food out for it and would never harm it.

Part of the isolated ruins of Sumharam

SUMHARAM AND KHOR RORI

The only site in Dhofar that dates to before Christ, Sumharam was the greatest city of southeast Arabia in 1000 BC, port for the frankincense trade route inland through Arabia to Jerusalem, Alexandria and even Rome.

Ancient harbour

The fenced-in ruins of Sumharam stand today isolated and forgotten, the fine limestone walls overlooking the silted-up natural harbour of Khor Rori. Before rockfalls and silt blocked its mouth, this was a safe harbour for ships from the Red Sea, Mesopotamia and the Far East. Now cut off from the sea by a sandy bank, the creek itself is freshwater, frequented by many migratory seabirds as well as

TRADE ROUTES

Known in ancient times as Moscha, Sumharam was the easternmost of the cities on the frankincense route, ruled by the kings and queens of Sheba and Yemen who controlled the myrrh of Yemen and the frankincense of Dhofar. From this ancient city, recorded as the greatest spice centre on earth, camels would transport the bags laden with frankincense first over the deserts to Damascus and Alexandria, then onwards to India and even as far as China. The Queen of Sheba herself decided on the actual course of the trade routes.

flamingoes. The whole area is totally deserted, making an excellent spot to camp in magnificent surroundings.

The ruins

The American academic Wendell Phillips was the first to excavate the site in 1952, but there are no excavations currently going on. Phillips found evidence of an impregnable fortress city dedicated to a pagan god. The temple of the Moon God 'Sin' guarded the frankincense stores here. The whole city is built from well-crafted limestone blocks, and from finds of bronze coins, amphorae and sculptures it has been dated to 100 BC.

Frankincense resin, the most important commodity in Sumharam

SHEBA'S PALACE

On the main gate of the city there are two glass cases enclosing the remaining inscriptions found *in situ*. Written in the old southern Arabian language and script of Himyaritic, they document the construction of the city that was built under the orders of a Sabean king for the purpose of controlling the frankincense trade and collecting it for export. The Sabean capital in the Yemeni region of Hadramaut was called Shabwa, from where the Queen of Sheba is thought to have got her name. Consequently, the site is sometimes also called Sheba's Palace.

Moon temple

Dedicated to the Moon God 'Sin', the central temple area is approached by a ramp of steps, and contains a well 30m (98ft) deep, now covered with protective bars. Its outer walls are 2.5m (8ft) thick in places. Many storage rooms were also found with incense still in them. Three sacrificial altars have been unearthed towards the sea end of the temple in a sunken area. On one of these altars there is a relief carving of a bull, one of the forms in which the Sabeans worshipped their lunar god. Around the altars the sacrificial remains of chicken bones, fish and birds were found, together with incense residue.
Open: Sat–Wed 7.30am–2.30pm. Closed: Thur & Fri.

MIRBAT

The tarmac road east from Salalah ends at Mirbat, a little fishing village on the
(*Cont. on p116*)

Frankincense

The region's name 'Arabia Felix' (Happy) came about because of the happiness brought by the riches earned through its frankincense, a valuable gum burned at religious ceremonies. In the days when the substance was used in temples and at funerals throughout the world, the Temple of Jerusalem had sacred rooms to store frankincense. The famous words of the *Song of Solomon* run: 'I will get me to the mountain of myrrh, and to the hill of frankincense.'

Ancient commodity

The writers of ancient Greece and Rome, such as Herodotus, Ptolemy, Pliny, Strabo and Diodorus, recorded how frankincense from Dhofar was taken by sea to all parts of the globe, and it has even been mooted that it was the first commodity to warrant the creation of international trade routes. It was said that the Queen of Sheba, for whom Dhofar was a colony, visited King Solomon in Jerusalem purely in order to agree a safe route for the frankincense caravans. The Romans under Augustus attempted in 24 BC to conquer the frankincense-producing countries, but were driven back

by thirst, unable to cross the vast Empty Quarter. In the 1st century AD, frankincense made the countries of southeast Arabia the richest in the world. Frankincense is produced only here and in Somalia, but the Arabian type is acknowledged to be better. At the peak of production 2,000 years ago, over 3,000 tons of frankincense was exported by camel caravan to the wealthy civilisations of Egypt, Greece, Rome and India.

Different types

There are four distinct types of frankincense tree. The best quality comes from the furthest inland, about

Traditional pottery incense burners

three days' camel journey from the coast, while the inferior types are found near the coast. The best is said to come from Hadhbarm, Sawdah and Mirbat, and the worst from Qushm. The tree itself is distinctive, growing to only 3 or 4m (9 to 13ft), gnarled and unattractive with hardly any leaves.

Harvesting technique

Small incisions are cut into the bark between March and August to allow the milky sap to seep out, taking three to five days to dry. The historian Pliny said that only a small number of privileged families were permitted to carry out the harvesting and tending of the trees: 'These persons are called sacred, and are not allowed, while pruning the trees or gathering the harvest, to receive any pollution, either by intercourse with women or contact with the dead; by these religious observances it is that the price of the commodity is so enhanced.' (*The Letters of Pliny the Younger*, Penguin Classics, 1969.) One tree can produce up to 20kg (44lb) a season. Today, the technique is less well understood, and inexperienced harvesting can lead to heavy damage of trees.

Incense burners

In recent years, the traditional hand-painted pottery frankincense burner

A frankincense tree in the Dhofar region

(*mejmarr*) has regained popularity after being used as packaging for Amouage's new perfume 'Salalah'. The pottery is made by Dhofari women who then paint it themselves in bright colours, giving a valuable boost to their family income. The burners come in all shapes and sizes and make unusual craft souvenirs or even Christmas gifts.

far headland of a long sandy beach. On the approach to the village, a sign points to the right towards Mirbat Castle, a fort overlooking the harbour, still with a group of three cannons in front defending against invaders from the sea. The fort is worth visiting for its views from the towers. There are also a few imposing old merchant houses left, with fine carved doors and windows, but they are decaying fast as their inhabitants move to nearby modern houses that are easier to maintain. The name Mirbat means 'place of tethering' in Arabic, a reference to the fact that this was a centre for exporting horses as well as frankincense.

A dilapidated structure in Mirbat

MOUNTAINS OF THE MOON

After Mughsail, the road westwards embarks on a stunning one-hour climb to the plateau of Jebel Qamr, Mountains of the Moon. Look out for the frankincense trees on the hillsides as the hairpin bends wind their way up and down the first chain of mountains. Near the summit there is a good stopping place with a series of little tracks leading off towards the sea. Here, you can enjoy magnificent views of the coastline and relax with a picnic.

70km (43 miles) east of Salalah. Fort. Open: Sat–Wed 8.30am–2pm. Closed: Thur & Fri.

Mughsail Blowholes

Mughsail beach is a magnificent 4km (2¹/₂-mile) stretch of white sand framed by spectacular cliffs at either end. On the further side is the wide, silted-up creek of Khor Mughsail, its pasture land enjoyed by grazing camels and cattle which are joined by many seabirds, as well as flamingoes, pelicans and storks. Immediately opposite the creek is the sign to Kahf Al-Marnaf. You can park beside the restaurant and tourist complex and enjoy the short walk along the path to reach the blowholes, which are not visible from the road. Grouped about 200m (220yds) past a cave and down the steps, the blowholes are at their most impressive during the summer monsoon season when the sea is at its fiercest. The blowholes are still active at other times of year but only at high tide. If your visit coincides with low tide, you will have to content yourself with only hearing the sea slopping about under the rocks, with the occasional soft roar and gentle spray forcing its way up through the metal safety grids, still enough to completely soak you, so keep cameras and suchlike well covered. *Mughsail beach is a comfortable half-hour's drive west from Salalah.*

Wadi Dirbat

East of Salalah beyond Taqa, a bridge crosses one of Dhofar's greenest wadis.

During and immediately after the monsoon rain, Wadi Dirbat is a tremendous sight, with lakes, pools and waterfalls and verdant pasture. During the rest of the year, it is worth visiting by four-wheel drive to see the dramatic gorge scenery of the upper reaches of the wadi, and its caves and their stalagmites and stalactites. One small cave even has some coloured animal paintings.

Staggering feats of engineering have been achieved in the Mountains of the Moon

Drive: Ubar, Atlantis of the Sands

Legendary frankincense city of the desert, Ubar is one of those places guaranteed to capture the imagination. After exploring it, you can have a picnic lunch in the desert to give you a taste of the silence and sand of the Empty Quarter, and return via the Pools of Ayoun and Job's Tomb.

An early start is usually made for visits to Ubar. A four-wheel drive vehicle is not strictly necessary to reach it as the graded track is very smooth and in good condition. Punctures are the main problem because the track has many small stones – make sure tyres are not under-inflated.

The site of Ubar lies northwest of Thumrait, 180km (112 miles) or 1³/₄ hours' drive from Salalah. Leaving Salalah by the main Muscat road, the flat coastal plain is soon crossed and the climb begins up the Qara mountains.

1 Qara mountains

Cows and camels are a common sight on the climb up the mountains, and they appear to wander freely in search of pasture with no sign of their owners. On the summit of the plateau, the landscape quickly reverts to featureless gravel desert.

At Thumrait, you reach a major crossroads from which roads head east into the oilfields around Marmul, and the graded track to Shisr (ancient Ubar) is clearly signposted as 72km (45 miles) to the left. Take this track; the journey is 45 minutes from here if you travel at 90kph (56mph). The Thumrait Hotel and Restaurant stands over to the right.

2 Ubar

A sudden outcrop of trees and buildings in the middle of the bleak landscape marks your arrival at Ubar. The fenced site is looked after by a resident guardian who lives in the adjacent housing estate which was built by the Sultan in 1970 with a school and mosque to encourage the nomadic population to settle. Approaching the site from above is the best way to appreciate how the heart of the city was said to have collapsed into this sinkhole. The *Arabian Nights* tells how God punished the city for its corruption and immortality, like Sodom and Gomorrah, making it fall in on itself and disappear into the sand. Sir Ranulph Fiennes' book, *Atlantis of the Sands*, is a must for the full fascinating story.

Returning from Ubar, you can vary the route by turning right towards Ayoun at the crest of the ridge of the Qara mountains. After about 20 minutes, Ayoun is signposted 6km (3¾ miles) to the right.

3 Pools of Ayoun

Thought to be the water source for Ubar, the green, tranquil pools lie at the foot of the gorge and it takes about 15 minutes to clamber down to them.

There are frankincense trees scattered by the parking area.

Continuing the descent from the Qara mountains, after 20 minutes a fork turns right to Job's Tomb, Nabi Ayoub.

4 Job's Tomb

The walled tomb enclosure is attractively set in a cluster of trees. Beyond it there is a café with stunning views from its terrace, which are especially fine at sunset.

The descent continues through extraordinary ravines and plateaux to reach the Salalah plain after 40 minutes' drive.

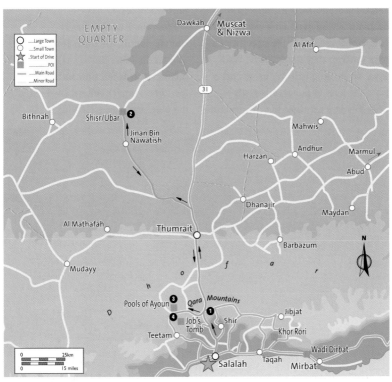

Getting away from it all

For the adventurous spirit, Oman is blessed with many remote places to explore, some of them quite challenging even to reach. The following pages describe a range of these, in the mountains, in the wadis and in the desert, but the list is far from exhaustive.

THE BATINAH COAST
Hawra Burgha

Hawra Burgha (*see map p62*) is a 13th-century fortress stronghold sited dramatically by itself, far away from all current habitation on the summit of a rock outcrop that straddles the Wadi Jizzi. An exciting half-day excursion from the base of Sohar, it is easily driveable in a car since the construction of a wide-graded track to the Wadi Jizzi dam. However, after heavy rains, the wadi crossings may require four-wheel drive.

From the Falaj Al-Qubail roundabout on the main Sohar to Muscat dual carriageway, take the road inland towards Buraimi and follow it for some 13km (8 miles). Turn left at the blue sign marked left for Wadi

Wadis usually have graded tracks leading in to them

Climbing up to Hawra Burgha

we get our word 'park'), a reference to the complex network of water channels, dams and cisterns that can still be seen. These would have enabled the inhabitants to irrigate their crops and be self-sufficient in the event of siege. In its heyday, the various terraces and levels must have been lush with vegetation, testament to the fact that rainfall was clearly high enough to sustain life on this magnificent hilltop. *Half-day excursion from Sohar. Allow about 1 hour to look around the deceptively large city stronghold. There is no shade on the summit, so it is wise to avoid the midday period.*

Lusail copper mine

Now utterly abandoned, this is the most spectacular of Oman's copper mines, still mined until as recently as the 1980s. A half-day outing from Sohar (*see map p62*), this excursion is very memorable and is a long way from any habitation, guaranteeing a peaceful and novel picnic spot. Like Hawra Burgha, it lies inland in the Wadi Jizzi which is famous for its ancient copper mines, to the left of the main road inland towards Buraimi from the Falaj Al-Qubail roundabout. There is no sign to Lusail from the main road but the landmark is the tall chimney stack of the modern copper smelting factory. About 1km (^{2}/$_3$ mile) further on from this, look out for the old tarmac road on the left that runs parallel to the main road. Take this road and then turn right, crossing the first wadi, then

Jizzi dam 4km (2^1/$_2$ miles). If you are sharp-eyed, you will notice along the ridges on both sides of the road a series of stone-built beehive tombs, more than 50 of them. Ignore the left turn-off to the dam itself and continue straight along the wide-graded track that crosses the wadi stream twice before arriving at the foot of the distinctive outcrop.

Parking at the point where the track passes closest to the rocky mound, the ascent on foot takes about 15 minutes and involves scrambling up the loose stones to cross a breach in the walls and reach the summit.

The name Hawra means 'white limestone' in Arabic, and Burghah means 'garden' in Persian (from where

Lusail copper mine

up and over a hill with a small cluster of portakabins to the left. Continue straight over the second wadi crossing and stop when you arrive at a dead end with 'DANGER NO ENTRY' signs.

The ancient mining galleries at Lusail were dug to a depth of 88m (289ft) below ground and were anything up to 30m (98ft) long, their roofs supported by acacia wood and date palm. As you stroll around the whole mining area, you will notice many examples of turquoise/green copper underfoot, as well as some fool's gold, properly known as copper pyrite, a mix of copper, iron and sulphur. Bright and yellow when freshly unearthed, it quickly tarnishes with exposure. A striking rock arch that you may have seen in photos is a ten-minute walk further on. On the way, look out for a few intriguingly sealed-off mine shafts. *Half-day outing from Sohar.*

EASTERN PROVINCE (SHARQIYAH)
Lizq

In the Sharqiyah, this unusual and remote Iron Age archaeological site is reached by forking off the main road between Bidbid and Ibra where the sign points right to Sinaw, and then forks left to Lizq village (*see map p90*). The landscapes around Lizq are very attractive, with small, almost volcanic-looking hills, very good for picnicking or even camping. The site itself is approached by a dramatic ceremonial stone staircase, unique in Oman, leading to a fortified citadel on the summit. The 79 steps that remain of the staircase present no particular difficulty, but the final 30m (100ft) or so to reach the summit, after the stairs run out, need care and sure-footedness because the rocks are loose and slippery. The villagers know the place locally as Jebel Ghaddaniya.

The best approach to the archaeological site is to drive through the centre of the modern village of Lizq, cross straight over the tiny roundabout, then follow the track as it bears left and traverses a small humped bridge. Whenever you are faced with two tracks, keep to the right, as the dirt road winds through the plantations between high mud walls. To the left, raised up on a rocky outcrop, you pass a small round watchtower. This is followed by a right-angle dog-leg turn before you continue straight on and out of the village. Once you are on the outskirts of the village sprawl, fork left, heading towards the hill that stands by itself immediately to the left of the large date plantation, about 1km (²/₃ mile)

beyond the edge of the modern village. A carefully driven car will cope with any of the tracks, and it does not matter which you take as long as you are aiming for the hill itself. As you get closer and approach the parking area at the foot of the hill, the stone staircase is readily visible climbing steeply up the centre of the hill.

The sides of the steps are framed by a low wall, and where the stairs end and the ground flattens out a little, the foundation remains of two small towers can be distinguished, guarding the entry point to the fortified summit. There is no obvious path from this point on, so you must simply pick whichever way seems easiest across the boulders and to the summit. It should

Mountains at the northern end of the Sharqiyah

take no more than 15 minutes to reach the summit. Once there, you are rewarded with stupendous views over the surrounding volcanic landscape – the hilltop site was chosen to command the land in all directions. Not much remains on the summit beyond a few stone-built rooms and fortifications, most of them concentrated on the far side of the summit to protect the site where the ground begins to drop away.

Masirah Island

Oman's largest island at about 70km (43 miles) in length, Masirah sits just south of the Wahhiba Sands, 20km (12^1/$_2$ miles) offshore (*see map p90*). The island makes a perfect getaway destination for a few nights, and has many untouched beaches. There is just one hotel, the 18-room Masirah Hotel (*tel: 25 504401*), which was built in 2005 and has a licensed restaurant.

The waves on the eastern side of the island are perfect for surfing and windsurfing. Reaching between 1–2m (3^1/$_3$–6^1/$_2$ft) high, the waves are at their highest from June to September. Camping on the beaches is good and there are some little shops where you can buy your essentials. The main island occupations are weaving and making fishing nets.

A full day's drive from the Capital Area. The island is reached by a 1-hour car ferry crossing from Ras Al-Najdah on the mainland. The ferry runs about four times a day at times that depend on the tides, and there is a charge.

DHOFAR
Al-Wusta

This area of desert lies halfway to Salalah from Muscat (*see map p106*), literally in the middle of nowhere, and it is the ultimate getaway from everything modern and developed. It is the least populated area of Oman, and the very name Al-Wusta means 'the middle area' in Arabic, an accurate description of this chunk of central Oman that is neither north nor south. For the most part, Al-Wusta is featureless gravel desert, totally uninviting, and most people simply drive through as fast as possible en route to Salalah. However, for those with four-wheel drive, the area does have something to offer, namely the coast, undoubtedly Oman's most dramatic and unspoiled by virtue of its very inaccessibility. All the sights here are natural, with not a fort or historic building anywhere to be found.

A week of self-sufficient camping is required to appreciate these natural beauties fully. Choose the cooler winter months for this excursion as there is no shade to be found at all since there is no vegetation to speak of. The minimum time is two nights away from the Capital Area, and you need to be totally self-sufficient in food, water and fuel. What petrol there is locally is often sold from oil drums in the villages.

The beaches of Ras Madraka are especially fine, with stretches of white sand broken up by contrasting black volcanic rocks and cliffs, and even by the rusting hulks of shipwrecks, stuck forever on the beaches where they were washed up. Two further unique spots are the pink lagoons near the village of Qahal, caused by resident algae, and a box canyon with sheer white cliffs at Shuwaymah quite unlike any other in Oman.

A minimum trip of two nights from the Capital Area.

Footprints in the sand, Shangerela beach

When to go

The best months to visit are November, December, January, February and March, with November probably the best of all, as the temperature never exceeds 32°C (90°F) and never falls below 22°C (72°F). The other bonus of this time of year is that the sea temperature is still pleasantly warm for swimming, while in December, January, February and even March, the sea is just a touch chilly for most people.

There are also marked variations from one part of the country to another, and the mountainous interior is much more bearable in the hot summer months than the coast with its stifling humidity. Muscat, hemmed in by mountains on the coast, is one of the hottest capitals in the world.

Dhofar (*see p106*) in the south is different again, and is subject to its own microclimate, catching the edge of the East African monsoon. The climate here around Salalah (*see p108*) is much more stable, with no such extremes as in the north of the country, and keeps to around 28°C (82°F) all year round. The best time to visit the Salalah area is mid-September, when the rains of the monsoon that began in mid-June are finishing, leaving a phenomenally green and beautiful landscape that lasts for just a few weeks. October is wonderful, but by early November the greenery has

virtually gone. Not surprisingly, this is peak season for Dhofar, and the Salalah hotels get very full with other Gulf Arabs as well as northern Omanis, for whom the contrast with their own much hotter climates is very marked. At other times prices drop much lower and the hotels have plenty of room.

In northern Oman rain can fall anytime between October and March, and sometimes even in the summer months, though this is unusual. Rain tends to be sudden and heavy. This can cause flash floods in the mountains that will then block the roads for a time where the wadis cross the main highways, as they do in many places, both on the Batinah Coast (*see p62*) and inland, as the water runs off the Jebel Akhdar range. Wadi crossings are marked by metal posts painted red at various heights at the side of the road in the run-up to the crossing, with road

Lovely beaches are commonplace in Oman and rarely busy

signs announcing 'stop when at red', i.e. when the water is so high it has reached the red mark. December and January tend to be the wettest months in northern Oman.

High-season prices in northern Oman apply from mid-October to mid-March, when the good hotels need to be booked well in advance. If you are prepared to come out of high season in the hotter summer months, especially June and July which are the lowest season, prices drop accordingly and you will have the hotel facilities more to yourself, which in the swimming pool will be especially welcome.

WEATHER CONVERSION CHART

25.4mm = 1 inch

$°F = 1.8 \times °C + 32$

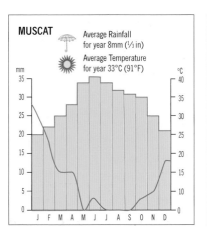

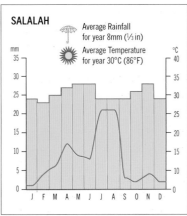

Getting around

Seeb International Airport (tel: 24 519223) will be the entry point for most visitors, and the average taxi fare from there into Muscat or Qurum is RO10. It takes about 30 minutes to cover the 40km (25 miles) on excellent dual carriageways.

By air

If travelling internally, there are domestic airports at Salalah, Sur and Khasab (in Musandam), serviced only by Oman Air, the national carrier (*Muscat. Tel: 24 707222. www.oman-air.com*). The timetables can be perused at their website.

By car
Self-drive car hire

Driving in Oman is easy and pleasant because traffic is not heavy, especially outside the Capital Area where roads can be relatively empty. Therefore, self-drive is recommended as by far the most enjoyable and flexible way of seeing the country, and it allows you to take advantage of all the wonderful places to stop and picnic en route.

There are many car-hire companies, including the big names like Hertz, Europcar, Budget and Avis, usually based at the big hotels and at the airports. Drivers need to be over 21 and show their passport, driver's licence (your national one is fine, there is no need to get a special international licence from the AA), and a credit card for the returnable deposit. For small cars, weekly rates are around RO80–RO110 and daily rates RO12–RO16, including full insurance and local taxes. It is usually possible to drive the car across the border into the United Arab Emirates, but make sure your car-hire company has been informed so that the insurance is extended to cover this. Keep all documentation in your glove compartment so that it can

FOUR-WHEEL DRIVE HIRE

Rental costs for four-wheel drive vehicles are far more expensive than normal car hire, at around RO40 a day. Unless you are experienced, you should certainly not attempt sand driving in a lone vehicle. As a visitor on holiday here, if you want to go off-road properly, it would better and far safer to go on an arranged tour through one of the many tour companies offering such trips.

Taxis are to be found all over the country

be shown to police if requested. In the event of an accident, the police must be summoned and the vehicle cannot be moved until they give the go-ahead.

The road system in Oman is good, with dual carriageways running up the length of the coast from Muscat to the United Arab Emirates border (a four-hour drive). Road signs are clear and in both English and Arabic. The speed limit is 120kph (75mph) on the dual carriageways and 60kph (37mph) in towns. Roundabouts are a common feature and far more numerous than traffic lights. Driving is on the right so all cars are left-hand drive.

Petrol is incredibly cheap and it costs only RO5 to fill a small car and RO15 to fill a four-wheel drive. Petrol stations are plentiful and usually have toilet facilities, if rather basic, and sometimes a little shop attached to get snacks, drinks and sweets. It is compulsory to wear your front seatbelt, and there is a RO10 fine if you are found not doing so. A lot of hire cars do not have rear seatbelts. Night driving outside the towns can be a little hazardous due to wandering camels, donkeys and goats.

By long-distance coach

Long-distance coaches are the cheapest way of travelling between cities. From the Ruwi Bus Station near Muscat, you can catch a coach south to Salalah, inland to Nizwa, to Ibra and Sur in the Sharqiyah (Eastern Province), and north to Sohar,

RAMADAN RESTRICTIONS

Only go to Oman during Ramadan if you are not bothered about drinking alcohol with your meal, as the hotels are not permitted to serve alcohol in the restaurants during this time. Alcohol is still available through room service in the privacy of your room, but not if you want to enjoy a leisurely bottle of wine with your friends over your meal. You may also find that without pre-booking you cannot eat in the hotels during Ramadan as they only cater for pre-booked guests.

Buraimi, and you can even cross into the United Arab Emirates and on to Dubai and Abu Dhabi. Coaches usually need to be booked a few days in advance to guarantee a seat, but you can get on without a reservation if there is room. The air-conditioned coaches are quite small, taking about 40–45 people, but they are comfortable enough. They stop at regular intervals at pre-arranged places, such as Seeb International Airport. No food or drink is provided so it is advisable to bring your own provisions for the journey.

The state-owned coach company is called Oman National Transport Company (*Muscat. Tel: 24 492948. www.ontcoman.com*) and details of its full timetable can be found on its website. The Salalah Express runs four times a day and takes 13 hours (*single adult fare of RO12 and a return fare of RO18; children under 12 travel half price*).

In addition to the state-owned company, there is a privately owned coach company called Comfort Line

(*Muscat. Tel: 24 702191*) that specialises in services to Dubai. These run twice a day, crossing into the United Arab Emirates at the Hatta Border Post where free visit visas are issued on the spot. The coaches used are, as the name implies, slightly more comfortable than the state-owned ones.

By taxi

Taxis are frequent, with honest and reliable drivers, and are by far the best means of transport for short distances within towns and the Capital Area. With their orange and white colouring, they are very conspicuous. Taxis are not metered, but in practice this is rarely a problem as the fares are very reasonable and you are unlikely to be overcharged. Tipping is not expected. In Muscat and the Capital Area, taxis can be pre-booked through your hotel. Chauffeur-driven limos can also be arranged through the luxury hotels for any special occasion, although this is obviously much more expensive.

By train

There are no trains at all in the Sultanate of Oman.

By white minibus

Mainly used by the immigrant workforce, these white vans/minibuses are sometimes called baiza buses because of their cheapness (the fare is only a few baizas). They ply the main highways in and around the towns and up the coastal dual carriageway, and can be hailed anywhere along their route, running randomly and filling randomly as they go.

Taxi rank in Muscat

Accommodation

Oman offers a range of accommodation from camping to luxury, but there is something of a gap in between. There are not really any formal campsites in the sense understood in the West, but you can camp freely anywhere, from the beach to the wadis, the deserts and the mountains. At the other end of the scale, Oman is particularly well endowed with hotels in the 4- and 5-star categories, including one of outstanding distinction, the Al-Bustan Palace (see p162), widely acknowledged as one of the best hotels in the Middle East, if not the world.

That said, prices are nowhere near as high as in Europe, and even the top-class hotels can be affordable (in the RO80–RO135 range), but you can still pay RO350 for a luxury suite if you want to splash out. The mid-range hotels cost from RO40–RO80, while some of the budget hotels offer rooms for as little as RO15.

Muscat and the Capital Area

By far the largest numbers of hotels are concentrated in the area around Muscat and the bays to the south of it. The big international chains such as the Intercontinental, the Crowne Plaza, the Hyatt and the Sheraton have prime locations on the beaches north of Muscat around Qurum (*see p163*), with a couple of ultra-exclusive hotels like the Al-Bustan Palace and the Shangri-La in their own bays to the south (*see pp162 & 161*). The business hotels are clustered in and around

Ruwi, the business and commercial district just north of Muscat. Muttrah is unusual in that it has a group of low-cost hotels along its corniche. The

The grand foyer of Al-Bustan Palace Hotel

Nizwa's Golden Tulip Hotel

middle 3-star category is less well served, with only a handful of places in the Ruwi business district, or the suburbs of Qurum north of Muscat, or near Seeb where the international airport is located. The drive from Seeb International Airport into Muscat and the main hotels takes about 30 minutes, or 40 minutes if you are going a little further south to the Al-Bustan Palace or the Shangri-La.

The interior and the south

Once you leave the Capital Area, there is a dearth of good accommodation. Along the Batinah coast there are just two places, one at Sohar and another at Al Sawadi (*see pp166 & 167*), while inland the only hotels are in and around Nizwa. En route to Sur and to Salalah is a handful of simple resthouses to break the journey, while in Salalah itself there is a group of luxury hotels on the beach (*see pp170–71*).

BOOKING AHEAD

Hotels get quite full during the high season period from mid-October to mid-March, and it is advisable to book ahead. Even outside these months, it is best to reserve in advance for Thursday and Friday nights – the Omani weekend – as many expatriates take weekend breaks throughout the year. Ramadan itself can be a little quieter, but the two *Eids* (religious holidays) are like the West's Christmas and Easter and get extremely busy. Always try asking for a discount, as many hotels will give one on demand.

Food and drink

Omani cuisine is very difficult to come by in restaurants, but some of the international hotels make an effort to offer one or two items just to show willing. The reason for this absence seems to be a combination of the fact that chefs in Oman are almost all Indian, and that ethnic Omanis eat out very rarely. As a result, by far the best and cheapest way to eat out is at the many Indian restaurants, most of which are not licensed. Alcohol is served only in the middle-range hotels and upwards, where the food tends to be international, Lebanese, Italian or Chinese.

Capital Area

The Capital Area offers by far the biggest number and range of eating options, from simple coffee-shop style restaurants to the exclusive restaurants that are mainly found in the 5-star hotels. As with the accommodation, the area least well served is the middle range of restaurants. The lower end consists mainly of cheap and cheerful Indian restaurants – simple places that serve no alcohol and where the curries are very good value. If you want alcohol with your meal, you will have to eat in a 3-star or above establishment.

OMANI CUISINE

Conspicuous by its absence from most restaurant menus, Omani food can be elusive. There is, however, one small chain called Bin Ateeq that does offer traditional local dishes in traditional style and surroundings, with seating on floor cushions. At present, the chain has three restaurants – in Muscat (at Al-Khuwair), Nizwa and Salalah (*see pp160, 165 & 171*). There is also a handful of traditional Omani cafés in the *souk* (market) at Muttrah. Omani cuisine is very simple, usually dry-cooked lamb (or more likely goat), flavoured with a few gentle spices and served with plain rice. The most any restaurants claiming to offer Omani food usually have on the menu is a couple of these main-course dishes, which tend not to be to European taste, with the meat on the tough side.

Most Omanis do not drink alcohol, so there is no locally produced wine or beer. Everything has to be imported and so prices are high. Typical beers available are Carlsberg, Tuborg, Heineken, Amstel, Budweiser and Fosters at around RO2 a bottle, with a small range of French, German, Italian, Californian and Australian wines costing RO10–RO20 depending on quality. Omanis themselves tend to drink water or fizzy soft drinks with their food, and tea without milk but lots of sugar and Arabic coffee in between meals. There is no drinking culture in Oman and the bars that exist are all within the confines of the upper-class hotels.

Inland and elsewhere

Once outside the Capital Area, as with the accommodation, the range of eating establishments narrows and your choices are limited to simple places run by Indians, or to hotels that have the only restaurants where you will be served alcohol. You can pick up simple snacks like crisps, sweets and fizzy drinks at petrol station shops, but it is a good idea to stock up properly so that you are self-sufficient and can picnic

PRICES

At the lower-end establishments, a two-course meal will cost you RO5–RO7, while in the middle range you should expect to pay RO7–RO15, excluding alcohol. In the upper range of restaurants, generally in the 4- and 5-star hotels, you will not get away with under RO15 a head excluding alcohol, and RO20 is probably more realistic. Add in the alcohol and you will end up paying closer to RO25 for a really good meal including service and taxes.

Kitchen at Jabrin Fort

anywhere that takes your fancy if you are heading inland. Always make sure you have a large pack of mineral water bottles in the boot of the car, and make a trip to one of the supermarkets that always have an excellent range of fresh fruit and vegetables, bread, cheese, dips and prepared foods such as roasted chicken, little savoury pastries and so on. The two chains to look out for are Al-Fair and Lulu, both of which offer a huge selection.

Vegetarian options

As in the rest of the Middle East, vegetarians are very well served in Oman. In the Indian-style restaurants there is always a vegetable curry that has the virtue of being cheaper than the meat ones, and the range of mezes is generally heavily vegetarian with hummus and other dips, vine leaves and peppers stuffed with rice, various cheeses (none of them local), and copious salads. Most restaurants will also offer omelettes with a selection of fillings. Nuts are abundant, as is dried fruit like figs and dates, the ultimate nourishment. Take a pack of dates with you on your travels and you will never go hungry, although your teeth may suffer.

Tipping etiquette

It is usual to leave a 10 per cent tip in restaurants unless service is expressly included.

A traditional Omani kettle

Entertainment

Western-style entertainment is thin on the ground in Oman as the Omanis do not have a culture of going out to bars and nightclubs. Evening entertainment consists of visiting friends and relations, and daytime entertainment revolves around shopping, or at the weekends picnicking with the family in the countryside, anywhere where some greenery or water can be found.

As a result, any evening entertainment is to be found in the 4- and 5-star hotels, and most have a bar/nightclub with live music and dancing. The entertainers at these venues tend to be Filipinos, Indians or Arabs from other countries such as Lebanon or Egypt. Piano cocktail bars and belly dancing are laid on at some hotels. The belly dancing is not part of indigenous culture, but is provided as part of what western visitors expect on a visit to any Arabian country. The standards of dancing are nothing like those in the real centres of this art, such as Egypt. Unaccompanied women are advised not to attend the nightclubs or bars as their presence will be misinterpreted as availability.

Cinema

The Capital Area boasts four cinemas that show films in English, Arabic and Hindi. They are scattered about

The bar at the Al Bandar hotel at Barr Al Jissah

Traditional music and dance in Oman

between Seeb, Ruwi and Qurum Beach and cater mainly for Asian clientele. The staple fare is action movies with posters of graphic violence and torture figuring largely. Women are advised not to go to the cinema alone as this will be seen as inviting attention.

Concerts

The only classical music that is occasionally performed in Oman tends to take place in the auditorium of the Al-Bustan Palace Hotel (*see p163*) by visiting musicians or small ensembles doing the rounds of all the Gulf countries. Sometimes the other major hotels have visiting musicians, and these performances are advertised in advance through the English daily *Times of Oman* (*www.timesofoman.com*).

Theatre

There is very little theatre on offer here. A few travelling shows a year stop at the Muscat Intercontinental Hotel as part of their Middle Eastern touring programme, and the British Airways Theatre Company lays on about three performances a year. You can check in the English daily *Times of Oman* to see what shows coincide with your visit (*www.timesofoman.com*).

Traditional dances and music

Cultural events involving traditional dances and music on Omani instruments are usually featured in the annual festival held at the Qurum Park auditorium. Otherwise, dance and

Spectators at a wadi-driving contest

music forms part of traditional wedding celebrations in the interior that, if you are lucky, you may just happen upon. The *Eids* (religious festivals) are occasions where dancing takes place out on the streets in the inland towns and villages, usually just involving the men, and often with swords or sticks.

Other activities

The relative lack of conventional Western-style entertainment does not mean there is nothing to do in Oman – far from it. Exploration of the outdoors is in effect the substitute, and with 82 per cent of Oman consisting of desert and the remainder mountains and wadis, there is a great deal to explore. Apart from wadi driving, there is caving, rock climbing, mountain climbing and trekking (*see pp144–5*). There are also forts, castles and a few archaeological sites to explore, as well as wildlife and bird-watching.

Shopping

Shopping for souvenirs in Oman is a joy because you are spoiled for choice. There are items to cover all budgets, from exotic herbs and spices bought in the souk *(market), to Omani wooden chests and silver decorated* khanjars *(traditional curved daggers worn at the belt). There is also gold and silver Bedouin jewellery worn around the neck or ankle, and Maria Theresa silver dollars (the former currency before the Omani rial was introduced) at the expensive end of the range.*

Traditional pottery items are also good buys, such as mini-pots and forts that make good planters in your garden back home. Omani rose-water is renowned, and there are plenty of other perfumes made from sandalwood, musk and other exotica with names like 'Secret of the Harem' and 'Bride of the Desert'. Traditional clothing is fun, like *dishdashas* (full-length men's robes) that make very good dressing gowns or house robes back home. For consumables, Omani dates and cardamom-flavoured coffee are recommended.

Traditional *souks* (markets)

The best place to get most souvenirs is from one of the traditional *souks*. In the Capital Area, the Muttrah Souk just inland from the corniche (*see p35*) will provide you with the best selection of items, and wandering along the maze of alleyways is in itself an experience not to be missed. Outside the Capital Area, the next best traditional *souk* is at

Nizwa, where there is a good range of traditional souvenir shops. Bahla is best for pottery, and there are two workshops in the town. Salalah in the south has a good *souk* for jewellery and a few other Dhofari specialities such as frankincense and incense burners. Bargaining is expected in *souks*, and you should aim to knock at least 20–30 per cent off the first price.

Shopping malls

In the Capital Area, there are several Western-style shopping malls with a range of familiar shops such as Marks & Spencer, the Body Shop, Gap, Next and BHS (British Home Stores). The usual fast-food outlets have a presence in these malls, including the ubiquitous McDonald's, Burger King, Pizza Hut and KFC (Kentucky Fried Chicken). Most of these malls are in the Qurum area, and all are modern, air-conditioned and popular with locals and immigrants alike as welcome refuges from the heat.

They also sell computers, mobile phones, stereos and photographic equipment, but the prices are not as cheap as in neighbouring Dubai. There is no tax-free shopping in Oman.

Art and antiques

In the Capital Area, there are a number of specialist galleries stocking the work of local artists, such as the Yiti Art Gallery near the Sheraton and the Bait Muzna Gallery opposite Bait Al-Zubair Museum in Muscat. Near the Muscat Intercontinental, the Oman Heritage Shop is a non-profit organisation selling a range of traditional arts and crafts, well worth a visit for souvenirs at fixed prices.

Drinking coffee in the *souk* at Rustaq

Omani doors and chests

Omani doors and chests are highly distinctive decorative items that can be purchased at a variety of outlets and make excellent souvenirs of the country. Transportation is obviously an additional cost, but most shops will arrange shipment back to your home country.

Doors

The main entrance to a building, be it a door or gateway, often receives the greatest attention in Islamic architecture, a statement of wealth and grandeur where most of the decorative elements are concentrated. From the inside, the door is generally

The imposing doors of Al-Hazm Fort

totally plain. The wood used is usually imported teak or rosewood from India, as Oman does not grow wood that lends itself to fine carving.

The favoured motifs of Omanis were often the traditional floral patterns of roses, Oman's favourite flower. Alas, these days there is only a handful of Omani carpenters left and so most wood is now carved by Indians imitating local designs. The doors have recently become popular with expatriates who use them as coffee tables. Many craft shops now sell them already converted, with legs and glass tops added.

Colour and texture are the distinguishing features when examining a door that is offered for sale. Look for a dark wood with a deep redness to be sure the door is old rosewood or teak, anything up to 200 years old. Orange-coloured wood is younger. Some sellers may stain the doors darker to disguise their age, but this masks the grain of the wood. Also look out for giveaway signs of newness, like a sharp feel to the carving and edges. Older doors enjoy a smoother finish that comes from wear and exposure, and this is difficult to mimic. Metal doors in

Chest in the fort of Jabrin

brightly coloured paints are fast replacing the old doors, and so the supply is getting ever smaller.

Chests

The traditional Omani chest, called *mandoos*, was originally designed as a ship's chest to carry and store belongings aboard ships. The chests come in all shapes and sizes, from tiny ones for jewellery to huge ones that need at least two men to carry them. Old chests are increasingly difficult to come by, but new ones are made and sold as souvenirs, with the smaller sizes dominating for practical reasons of transportation. The *souks* (markets) at Nizwa and Muttrah have stalls offering good selections, all with the traditional metal studwork as decoration. One of the biggest collections of old chests in the country can be seen at Jabreen. This must have at least 50 chests in different sizes, styles and colours, which are scattered about in the various rooms of the palace.

TIMBER FROM MALABAR

All timber for Oman's ships and dhows had to be sourced from India, and on his re-creation of the Sindbad Voyage, Tim Severin did likewise, travelling 2,092km (1,300 miles) to the coast of Malabar to get timber for his ship *The Sohar*. Severin and his men made excursions into the forest to hand-pick the timber, called *aini*, which did not even need to be seasoned for boat building.

Sport and leisure

Beyond the usual hotel-based sports and leisure activities like tennis, swimming, golf, gyms, saunas and spas, Oman offers an impressive range of outdoor adventure sports – land-based in the mountains and wadis, and water-based on the beaches.

Land sports

Oman's wild and unspoiled terrain lends itself to adventure activities, most of which involve a degree of driving off-road and then camping. Having a four-wheel drive makes life easier but it is surprising how much can be done with a robust Japanese saloon car. When camping, always make sure you take plenty of water, as well as supplies of food that won't go off in the heat (dates and La Vache Qui Rit cheese are superb), insect repellent, first-aid kit, sun hat and comfortable bedding.

Caving and rock climbing

There are excellent specialist publications available locally on these activities, but the best areas for rock climbing are Jebel Misht, Jebel Ghul and Jebel Misfah, all in the Jebel Akhdar mountain range and accessible from a base of Nizwa. Some tour operators run organised groups with experienced guides (*see p166*).

Oman's finest cave is said to be Majlis Al-Jinn in the Sharqiyah near Ibra, with a main cave chamber bigger than the great pyramid of Egypt. Easier for the beginner are the Hoti Cave near Hamra and the Al-Kittan Cave near Ibri. Near Salalah in the south of the country, the Teyq Cave is one of the largest in the world.

Horse-riding

The Al-Sawadi Beach Resort has stables on the beach and offers a range of trails (*see p167*), and the Royal Stables at Seeb on the edge of the Capital Area offers lessons and trails as well (*see p65*). There is also an equestrian school inside Qurum Natural Park (*see p164*).

Mountain trekking

Unlike caving and rock climbing, this requires no special equipment beyond a good, comfortable pair of walking boots, and is a wonderful way to experience the stunning mountainous terrain Oman has to offer. If you have good maps and a global positioning system (GPS), you can undertake certain treks independently such as the walk around the rim of the Wadi Nakhr crater, Oman's Grand Canyon. If you prefer the safety of an organised group, there are tour operators that run a choice of itineraries with different ranges of difficulty. A certain level of fitness is essential, with strong knees and ankles for all the sharp ascents and descents. The local publication *Adventure Trekking in Oman* is worth investing in.

Spectator sports

Although football is widely played and each main town has its sports stadium, there is not much to watch. Instead, the traditional spectator sports of camel racing and horse racing are worth watching – these can both be seen at Seeb camel race course, and Salalah in the south also has a course. These tend to take place at the weekends and during *Eids* (religious festivals). Bullfighting is the other spectator sport to look out for along the Batinah Coast, in the villages between Barka and Sohar – bloodless competitions of strength between bull and bull, with no human involvement except to lead the bull into the open square (*see p67*). Dolphin- and whale-watching make pleasant and relaxing outings by boat, best done around Fahal Island near the Capital Area or in Musandam in the north. On these boat trips, sometimes you may be invited to try your hand at fishing Omani-style with a handline, and then you can cook your catch.

Marina just south of Muscat

Watersports

Oman's long and varied coastline provides superb opportunities for a variety of watersports, and there is an ever-increasing number of watersports centres generally attached to the major hotels. Those at the Al-Bustan Palace, the Hyatt Regency, the Muscat Intercontinental and the Al-Sawadi Beach Resort are particularly good and well equipped. Sailing and windsurfing are popular at the hotels.

Diving and snorkelling

Oman can boast 63 registered dive sites and, with the exception of Dhofar in the south during the June–September monsoon season, diving is possible all year round. Best of all are the spring and summer months that enjoy calm and settled waters when the water is at its clearest. Some of the big hotels like the Al-Bustan

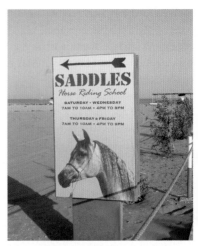

Horse-riding is available on the beach at the Al-Sawadi Beach Resort

Palace and the Al-Sawadi Forum Resort (*see p167*) offer diving packages with accommodation, and the cost includes the diving course itself, equipment hire and dive permits. In addition to the hotels, there are some independent diving centres such as the Oman Dive Centre and Bluzone (*see p161*). Courses from beginners to advanced are offered, and on successful completion the internationally recognised PADI (Professional Association of Diving Instructors) certificates are issued.

The best areas for diving are considered to be the Damaniyat Islands opposite the Al-Sawadi Beach Resort, a 45-minute drive north from Muscat, where courses, night dives and wreck dives can be arranged through the hotel. Other excellent spots are the eastern coastal bays

SEA HAZARDS

The dangers arising from sea animals are usually exaggerated out of all proportion. Although there are plenty of sharks in Omani waters, there has never been a recorded case of an attack on a swimmer, snorkeller or diver in Oman. The dangerous reef creatures are armed for their own protection and so are defensive not aggressive. If you step on a sea urchin or a stingray, they will hurt you, so be sure never to stand on coral, as you may cause yourself pain and damage the reef. Also avoid picking up cone shells because some of these carry a fatal poison. Floating peacefully above the reefs and watching the life below, your only danger will be potential sunburn.

south of the Capital Area such as Bandar Khayran and Bandar Jissah. Popular sites within 30 minutes of the Capital Area are the MS *Mimoona* wreck at Quriyat, Ras Abu Daoud, and Fahal Island. In other parts of Oman, the best dive sites are off the rocky bays of Musandam in the north and off the rocky shores of Dhofar in the south.

Snorkelling is of course far simpler and cheaper than diving, and requires no special fitness. As long as you can float, you can snorkel. Any stretch of rocky coastline is likely to yield plenty of fish to watch.

Camel racing

Children

Since so much of a holiday in Oman is geared to outdoor activity, adventure and beaches, children generally love it as a destination. However, there is very little by way of organised entertainment such as theme parks and special children's activities, but this makes the holiday a more challenging experience – children are less spoon-fed with entertainment and more at liberty to discover things to amuse themselves.

Beaches and seaside activities

All children will love the Omani beaches, which vary from long stretches of sand to rocky coves and bays. The sandy beaches have fine golden sand, perfect for digging and building sandcastles, while the rocky bays have good sea life that older children can enjoy watching while snorkelling. There are virtually no hazards in the sea and the currents are slight. If you want to be extra cautious, tell the children not to pick up any cone shells from the beach as a small number of these do have poisonous stings. You could also kit them out with plastic-soled sandals in the water to make sure they don't step on sea urchins or other spiny creatures on the rocks. The biggest hazard will be sunburn, so do make sure children are well protected, and try to keep them in the shade during the sun's fiercest hours between 11am and 3pm.

Playgrounds and parks

Omanis do enjoy strolling in parks among the greenery and flowers, and most parks are equipped with children's playgrounds that have swings, slides and seesaws. The Riyam Park in the Capital Area between Muscat and Muttrah is popular, as is the Naseem Garden out near Seeb (*see pp37 & 65*). The parks usually have public toilets and drinking-water stands. Older children will enjoy the challenge of trekking, and an easy trek begins immediately in front of the Riyam Park and is clearly signposted.

Children in restaurants

Omanis adore children, as do all Arabs, and there is no problem with taking children of all ages into restaurants, except perhaps the ultra-exclusive ones in the luxury hotels where they would feel out of place. Many of the hotels have buffet arrangements for breakfast, lunch and dinner, so there is bound to be something that children will find appetising. On the whole, as in all Arab countries, no special attempt is made to prepare food just for children. Children are simply expected to eat smaller portions of whatever the adults are eating. Arabs also love to eat with their fingers, and much Arab food is designed to do just that, so there is no need to stand on ceremony with cutlery. There is now a handful of fast-food outlets like KFC (Kentucky Fried Chicken), Pizza Hut and McDonald's, but these are regarded as overpriced and are not used much by local people who generally prefer fresh food. All the usual fizzy drinks like Coke and Fanta are available everywhere.

The shallow sandy beaches offer safe swimming for children

Essentials

Arriving

By air

Muscat International Airport, the arrival point for the vast majority of visitors, is located 40km (25 miles) north of Muscat and is a 30-minute drive from the Capital Area and the main hotels. It is currently in the process of expanding, adding a new terminal building and extra runway. The main airlines operating here are Gulf Air (25 per cent owned by Oman), Emirates, British Airways, Swissair, KLM and Air France, and of course the national carrier Oman Air which is expanding its network. As well as servicing European capitals, the airlines fly from Africa, Asia, Australia and the USA. Salalah Airport in the south receives international flights only from other Gulf Cooperation Council (GCC) countries, so other visitors who want to go to Salalah have to transfer to a domestic onward flight from Seeb. Oman Air, Gulf Air and British Midland are the only carriers to fly direct, taking seven hours from London, while Qatar Airlines has a short stopover at Doha, Emirates has a stopover in Dubai, and British Airways has a stopover in Abu Dhabi. Prices vary greatly depending on the season and how far in advance you are booking.

By land

Oman can only be entered by land from the United Arab Emirates because

it is not possible to drive across any border from its other neighbours of Saudi Arabia or Yemen.

There are six entry points from the United Arab Emirates. The procedures are fairly straightforward and the process usually takes around 20–30 minutes, depending on the volume of traffic. There are no restrictions on women travelling alone in their car. If crossing in a car hired in the United Arab Emirates, it is usually cheaper to arrange the insurance cover for Oman in advance through the hire company than to buy it at the border, although this is also possible. The most frequently used crossing point is the Hatta border post from Dubai (also called Al-Wajajah). The drive from Dubai to Muscat along the Batinah dual carriageway takes about four hours and is an unexciting journey, the only scenic part being immediately either side of the border post itself. There are two crossing points at Buraimi (one at Wadi Jizzi between Sohar and Buraimi and the other at Jebel Hafeet en route to Ibri and Nizwa), and one on the coast at Khatmat Milahah from Fujairah emirate. There are two more crossings in the north into Musandam, one from Ras Al-Khaimah emirate into Bukha and the other from Fujairah emirate into Dibba. If you fly into Dubai International Airport and then cross into Oman within 15 days, the visa fee of RO6 is waived. Leaving Oman and re-entering the United Arab Emirates is straightforward, with a free re-entry visa issued on the spot at the border.

By rail

There is no railway system in Oman.

By ship

There are no scheduled passenger services arriving in Oman, only cargo vessels docking at Muttrah and Salalah. Some cruise ships do day-trip stopovers at Khasab in Musandam in the north, Muttrah in the Capital Area and Salalah in the south. A high-speed passenger ferry now runs between Muscat and Musandam.

Customs

Firearms, narcotics and pornographic material are banned in Oman. If any overtly sexual material is found in luggage, it is confiscated. Up to 2 litres of alcohol (non-Muslims only), a reasonable quantity of tobacco, 227ml of perfume and five DVDs may be brought into the country. Alcohol is strictly forbidden in private vehicles at land-border crossings, and the vehicles of parties of expatriates travelling over from Dubai for weekends or holidays

are searched for it. If found, the alcohol is confiscated and you are fined heavily. Sometimes, great lengths are gone to by alcohol-dependent expatriates, with alcohol concealed inside thermos flasks or other apparently innocuous containers. There are no restrictions on camera equipment, computers or music players. On leaving the country, make sure you do not have any rhino horn or ivory on your *khanjar* (traditional dagger) because this is illegal to export.

Departure tax

Whether you leave by air or across one of the land borders, there is a compulsory RO5 departure tax for all nationalities. Make sure you keep back RO5 in Omani currency for this.

Electricity

Due to its close historic ties with Britain, Oman, unusually for a Middle Eastern country, has UK-type flat three-pin plugs.

Etiquette

As in all traditional Muslim societies, a decent standard of dress is expected. Both sexes should confine shorts to the beach, and women should make sure that their upper arms and their legs to the knee are covered. Wear loose clothing; anything else is seen as provocative. Always ask permission before taking photos, especially of women. Non-Muslims are not allowed to enter mosques (with one or two notable exceptions). During Ramadan, be sure not to eat, drink or smoke in public during daylight hours. Western women should keep eye contact with local men to a minimum because this is seen as inviting attention.

Health and pharmacies

No specific vaccinations are required in Oman, but typhoid and hepatitis A are recommended. Tap water is safe to drink, but safer still is the cheap and plentiful Omani mineral water. Muscat Pharmacy is the biggest chain of chemists, with well-stocked branches all over the country. In the Capital Area, a few are open 24 hours, and the details are given in the English daily *Times of Oman* (*www.timesofoman.com*).

Language

English is widely spoken in all shops and businesses, where around 80 per cent of shopkeepers are Indian, compared to 99 per cent in the neighbouring United Arab Emirates. Spoken Arabic in Oman is closest to the classical, written Arabic because there has been minimal foreign interference, but you will have to be quite determined to find opportunities to use it in the Capital Area. However, in the interior it is often the only language spoken, but most small children appear to have learned 'pen' and 'money' in English.

Written Arabic is everywhere on street signs and adverts, so there is plenty of practice for your Arabic alphabet. Like the other Semitic language to which it is closely related, Hebrew, Arabic is based on a root system of three consonants. It has only 29 characters and the short vowels are not written. Of the 29 consonants, 18 have direct English equivalents such as b, d, t, l and s, and others have near equivalents like the emphatic d, s, t and z, transliterated as capital D, S, etc. This leaves only a small handful that is genuinely difficult for Westerners to pronounce, notably the 'ain', a letter that sounds like a guttural constriction of the larynx, usually represented in transliteration by an inverted comma.

Media
Suggested reading

Oman and its Renaissance by Sir Donald Hawley (Stacey International, 2005) – the best general coffee-table book, with beautiful photos and intelligent text written by a former British ambassador to Oman.
Oman in Early Islamic History by I Al-Rawas (Ithaca Press, 2000) – a detailed study of Oman's history from the advent of Islam until 893.
Unknown Oman by Wendell Phillips (Librairie du Liban, 1966) – interesting read by this archaeologist and explorer who was involved in Oman's early digs.
The Making of a Modern State by John Townsend (St Martin's Press, 1977) – thought-provoking book that was initially banned in Oman as it was sailing too close to the wind.
The Voyage of Sindbad by Tim Severin (Putnam Publishing Group, 1983) –

fascinating account of Severin's re-creation of Sindbad's voyage to China, a mission sponsored by the Sultan.

Atlantis of the Sands by Sir Ranulph Fiennes (Bloomsbury, 1992) – story of Fiennes' quest for the lost city of Ubar on the edge of the Empty Quarter.

The Southern Gates of Arabia by Freya Stark (John Murray, 1936) – absorbing account of the author's journey to explore the Frankincense Road.

Arabia Deserta by Charles Doughty (Peter Smith Publishing, 1960) – travel classic describing two years spent with the Bedouin in the late 19th century.

Desert, Marsh and Mountain by Wilfred Thesiger (Flamingo, 1995) – classic account of five years spent with the Bedouin before the days of oil and modernity.

Local media

There are locally produced English books in Oman that provide excellent coverage of the country's natural history, wildlife, diving, sea life, adventure trekking, caving, off-road driving and climbing. These can be found in the hotel bookshops and in the Family Bookshop chain (*www.soukofoman.com/familybookshop.html*).

The English daily *Times of Oman* (*www.timesofoman.com*) has listings of entertainment and cultural events. There is also a good magazine, *Adventure Oman*, on local adventure activities, and *Oman 2day* (*www.apexstuff.com*), a small-format magazine with restaurant reviews and up-to-date information.

Oman television broadcasts in Arabic and English, and is controlled by the Ministry of Information. Radio Oman is state owned and also broadcasts in Arabic and English. The BBC World Service can be picked up at certain times, but for world news the better hotels have satellite television offering BBC World or CNN.

Money

The Omani rial is divided into 1,000 baizas. It is best to change money once inside the country as rates are better there. Rates of exchange are pegged to the dollar at RO1 = US$2.60 and are usually quite stable. ATMs (cash machines) are plentiful in the main towns throughout the country, and up to RO300 can be withdrawn per day. Credit cards are widely accepted in the larger hotels (3-star and upwards), but in petrol stations, smaller restaurants and *souks* (markets) you will need cash. If you prefer not to travel with cash, travellers' cheques should be American Express and in US dollars, but they can only be changed in the larger banks and hotels.

Opening hours

Government offices: *Open: Sat–Wed 7.30am–2.30pm.*
Banks: *Open: Fri–Wed 8am–1pm, Thur 8am–noon. Closed: Fri.*
Private sector: *Open: Fri–Wed 8am–1pm & 4–7pm, Thur 8am–1pm.*

Shopping malls: *Open: Sat–Thur 9am–1pm & 4–9pm, Fri 4.30–10pm.*
Souks (markets): *Open: Sat–Thur 8am–1pm & 4–9pm, Fri 4.30–9pm.*

Passports and visas

All visitors need a valid passport to enter Oman. On arrival at Seeb International Airport, a single-entry visa is issued which is valid for 28 days. The cost is RO6 for all foreigners, except Arabs from the Gulf Cooperation Council (GCC) states of Bahrain, Saudi Arabia, Qatar and Kuwait, who pay RO3. You can pay in foreign currency or by credit card, and if you pay in foreign currency cash, any change will be given to you in Omani rials. The same regulations apply if you cross from a land border, such as from the United Arab Emirates in the north, and the 28-day visa is issued on the spot and the costs are the same. For all nationalities, visas for under-18s are free. If you require a longer stay, you must apply for a one-year or two-year multi-entry visa that must be sponsored by your employer in Oman. The same rules apply to nationals of Australia, Canada, New Zealand, South Africa, the UK and USA. To check the latest details, visit *www.rop.gov.om* and *www.destinationoman.com*

Public holidays
Religious

The religious holidays are fixed according to the lunar calendar and move forward by about 11 days a year.

29 Dec 2009, 18 Dec 2010 – Islamic New Year (1st Muharram)
16 Feb 2010, 5 Feb 2011 – Prophet's Birthday (Mawlid An-Nabi)
22 Aug 2009, 11 Aug 2010, 1 Aug 2011 – Ramadan
21 Sept 2009, 10 Sept 2010, 30 Aug 2011 – Eid Al-Fitr (end of Ramadan)
28 Nov 2009, 16 Nov 2010, 6 Nov 2011 – Eid Al-Adha (end of the pilgrimage)

Non-religious

1 Jan – New Year's Day
23 July – Renaissance Day
18 Nov – National Day
19 Nov – Sultan's Birthday

Telephones and communication

The Oman country code, if calling from abroad, is 968 followed by the local number. Making international calls from Oman is cheaper between 9pm and 7am. Landline numbers are six digits with a two-digit area code. The area codes are:
24 for Muscat
23 for Dhofar
25 for the interior and the Sharqiyah (Eastern Province)
26 for Musandam.

Internet

Oman's internet service provider is Omantel, and all serious businesses have email addresses and their own websites. Bigger hotels have business centres where you can log on to check emails, and there are internet cafés scattered about in the main shopping areas of all major towns. These are widely used and popular with local youth.

Mobiles and Blackberries

Oman is on the GSM (Global System for Mobile), and all foreign mobile phones work fine. For communication within the country and back to your home country, SMS (Short Message Service) texting is the most cost-effective way, and works efficiently. Coverage is country-wide and the signal is usually strong even in the middle of nowhere. Frustratingly, Blackberries can receive emails but cannot, at the time of writing, send them.

Time

Omani time is GMT (Greenwich Mean Time) + 4 hours, making it 4 hours ahead of the UK in the winter months from November to March, and 3 hours ahead from April to October when the UK is on British Summer Time (BST).

Toilets

There is a dearth of public toilets in Oman. While travelling around in towns, your best bet is to use the hotels, which will generally have toilet facilities in their reception areas. Avoid using petrol stations where the facilities leave a great deal to be desired, especially for women. While in the countryside and outside the towns, the great outdoors is the cleanest and often the only option.

Travellers with disabilities

Wheelchair access is not obligatory for Oman's tourist facilities, but since most hotels were built post-1980, access is generally good and hotel staff are always delighted to help. Only the Chedi Hotel in the Capital Area (*see p160*) has pools with gradual steps instead of ladders, and as a rule the further you venture from the Capital Area, the more challenging things become.

Most signposts in Oman are bilingual

Language

RICH VOCABULARY

By the very nature of its structure, Arabic is an extremely rich language capable of expressing fine shades of meaning, a fact reflected in the wealth of Arabic literature, especially poetry. The average English tabloid reader is said to have a working vocabulary of 3,000 words, whereas the Arab equivalent has around 10,000. The written Arabic language, together with Islam, is one of the few unifying factors in the Arab world.

Like the other Semitic language to which it is closely related, Hebrew, Arabic is based on a root system of three consonants. It has only 29 characters and the short vowels are not written. Of the 29 consonants 18 have direct English equivalents such as b, d, t, l and s, and others have near equivalents like the emphatic d, s, t and z, transliterated as capital D, S etc here. This leaves just a small handful that are genuinely difficult for Westerners to pronounce, notably the 'ain', a letter that sounds like a gutteral constriction of the larynx, usually represented in transliteration by an inverted comma.

Everyday words and phrases

English	Arabic	English	Arabic
Hello, welcome	MarHaba, ahlan	Expensive	Ghaalee
Goodbye	Ma'a as-salaama	Money	Fuluus
Yes	Aiwa, na'am	Very, a lot	Katheer, waagid
No	Laa	No problem	Mush mushkila
Please	Min faDlak	Never mind	Ma'a laysh
Thank you	Shukran	Shop	Dukkaan
Sorry, excuse me	'Afwan, muta'assif	Open	MaftuuH
Hurry up, let's go	Yallah	Shut	Mughlag
Is it possible?		Bank	Bank, maSraf
May I?	Mumkin?	Chemist	Saydalia
How much		Ill, sick	MareeD
(does it cost?)	Bikaam?	Hospital	Mustashfaa
Cheap	Rakhees	Museum	MatHaf

English	Arabic	English	Arabic
Market	Souk	Jam	Murrabah
Police	ShurTa, buulees	Honey	'Asl
Airport	MaTaar	Bread	Khubz
Ticket	Tadhkara	Sugar	Sukkar
Suitcase	ShanTa	Vegetables	Khudra
Hotel	Fundug, ootel	Salad	SalaTa
Room	Ghurfa	Today	Al-yawm
Toilet, bathroom	Hammam, bait maa	Tomorrow	Bukra (in practice anytime between tomorrow and never)
Towel	Manshafa		
Soap	Saabuun		
Gents	Rijaal	Taxi	Taksee
Ladies	Sayyidaat	Car	Sayyarah
The bill	Al-Hisaab	Bus	Baas
Restaurant	MaT'am	Right	Yamen
Breakfast	FuTuur	Left	Yasaar
Lunch	Ghada	Straight on	Dhughri, 'ala Tuul
Dinner	'Asha	Far	Ba'eed
Glass	Kubbeyah	Near, close by	Gareeb
Wine	Khamr, nabeedh	Petrol station	MaHaTTat benzeen
Beer	Beera	Where?	Wayn?
Mineral water	Maa ma'daniya	What?	Shuu?
Coffee	Gahwa	Forbidden	Mamnuu'
Tea	Shay	Good	Zain
Eggs	BayD	Bad	Mush zain
Fish	Samak	Hot	Haar
Meat	LaHm	Cold	Baarid
Fruit	Fawaakah	If God wills, hopefully	In shaa Allah
Butter	Zabdah		
Cheese	Jubnah	Thanks be to God, thankfully	Al-Hamduu lillah
Yoghurt	Laban		

Emergencies

Telephone numbers
Fire: *999*
Royal Oman Police: Muscat *24 560099*;
Salalah *23 290099*
Royal Hospital: *24 592888*
AAA (car breakdown service): *24 605555*

Health
In the late 1960s, there were only three hospitals in the country and eight out of ten babies died within ten months of conception. Today, health care in Oman is excellent, but it is expensive for visitors and medical insurance is recommended. Simple precautions like drinking plenty of mineral water or soft drinks, avoiding the sun between 11am and 3pm, and wearing a sun hat and sunglasses will help to prevent the most common problems of sunburn and heatstroke. Malaria still exists in the inland wadis but the risk is tiny, and most people simply use insect repellent to avoid getting bitten. There are no compulsory vaccinations apart from yellow fever if you are arriving from an infected area.

Crime and safety
One of the safest tourist destinations in the world, crime rates in Oman are extremely low. As in all Muslim societies, assault and rape are virtually unknown since they would bring such dishonour to the family as to render them unthinkable. Petty crime like theft is rare but it does exist, although the perpetrators are far more likely to be Asian than Omani. Apply normal precautions such as locking your car and keeping your money out of sight.

Single women travellers can feel totally safe taking taxis, public transport, hiring a car or even walking alone at night on the streets of the Capital Area. The Omani temperament is relaxed and courteous, and provided your dress and demeanour are modest, you will have no difficulties at all.

Embassies
Most countries are represented in Oman, and embassy opening hours are Saturday to Wednesday 8am–2pm (closed Thursday and Friday). The majority is grouped in the diplomatic quarter behind Qurum Beach.

Australia
Australia does not have an embassy or consulate in Oman. Any assistance required by Australian nationals in Oman is provided by the Australian embassy in Saudi Arabia:
Abdullah bin Hozafa Al-Sahmi Ave, Diplomatic Quarter, Riyadh.
Tel: (966) 1 488 7788.
Canada (consulate)
Flat 310, Bldg 477, Way 2907, Mousa Abdul Rahman Hassan Bldg,

A'Noor St, Ruwi. Email:
canada_consulate_oman@hotmail.com

New Zealand (consulate)

PO Box 520, PC 113, Bldg No 387, Way No 3007, Muttrah.

Tel: 24 794932, 24 795726, 24 786039.

Fax: 24 706443.

UK

PO Box 300, PC 13, Jami'at Ad-Duwal Al-'Arabia St.

Tel: 24 693077, 24 609000.

Fax: 24 693087.

www.britishembassy.gov.uk/oman

USA

PO Box 202, PC 115, Madinat Qaboos

Tel: 24 698989, 24 699049.

Fax: 24 604316, 24 699778.

www.muscat.usembassy.gov

Emergencies

An embassy in the diplomatic quarter, Muscat

Directory

Accommodation price guide

★	Under RO20
★★	RO20–RO65
★★★	RO65–RO120
★★★★	Over RO120

Prices of accommodation are based on an average double room for two people sharing, including breakfast.

Eating out price guide

★	Under RO15
★★	RO15–RO20
★★★	RO20–RO30
★★★★	and ★★★★★
	Over RO30

Prices are based on the average cost of a meal for two without alcohol. Most of the upmarket restaurants that serve alcohol are to be found within the luxury 4- and 5-star hotels.

MUSCAT AND THE CAPITAL AREA
Al-Khuwair
ACCOMMODATION
The Chedi ★★★★★

A recent addition to the luxury class of 5-star hotels, the Chedi's location is not a patch on the Al-Bustan Palace (*see p162*). It is in the suburb of Ghubbra, just 10 minutes from the airport, with a rather bleak and sandy approach to the beachfront. The single-storey minimalist Zen style conveys a rather cold feel, with lots of silver, white and metal in the décor. The 261 bedrooms have showers, not baths. There are two tennis courts, two pools and a spa, but no watersports. Children under 16 are discouraged. Four restaurants are on offer, all very stylish and smart. *PO Box 964, PC 133. Tel: 24 524400, 24 524401. Fax: 24 493485, 24 504485. Email: chedimuscat@ghmhotels. com or reservation@ chedimuscat.com. www.chedimuscat.com*

EATING OUT
Automatic Restaurant ★★

Award-winning Lebanese food chain, also with branches in Qurum and Seeb. Good value. *Tel: 24 487200. Open: Sat–Thur noon–midnight, Fri 1pm–midnight.*

Bin Ateeq ★★

One of three, the others being in Nizwa and Salalah, this unlicensed restaurant is beside the Shell petrol station on the Al-Khuwair slip road. There is traditional Omani seating on cushions, with good value and authentic ambience. *Tel: 24 603225.*

The Red Lobster ★★

Near the Ministry of Tourism between Azaiba and Ghubbra, this is a good-value licensed restaurant with a large and varied menu. There is live music after 9pm. *Tel: 24 591993.*

The Restaurant ★★★★
There are four open-display kitchens here, cooking Arabic, Asian, Mediterranean and Indian food.
The Chedi Hotel.
PO Box 964, PC 133.
Tel: 24 524343.
www.chedimuscat.com

Sport and leisure
City Bowling
Opposite the Holiday Inn in Al-Khuwair. Tel: 24 541277.

Al-Khuwair Centre Ice Rink
Open: Sat–Thur 9am–8pm, Fri 11.30am–8pm.

Bandar Jissah Bay
Accommodation
Oman Dive Centre Beach Huts ★★
By itself on the road to the Al-Bustan Palace in Bandar Jissah bay, the Dive Centre offers fully equipped *barasti* (palm-frond) huts with air-conditioning. There is a licensed restaurant. The room rate includes breakfast and dinner.
Tel: 24 824241, 24 824240. Fax: 24 799600.

Barr Al-Jissah
Accommodation
Shangri-La's Barr Al-Jissah Resort and Spa ★★★★★
Opened in 2006, there are 680 rooms divided between three separate hotels here – Al-Waha for families; Al-Bandar for businesspeople; and Al-Husn, an exclusive 6-star place for the very rich. The resort is set in 50ha (124 acres) of landscaped gardens within its own bays with a mountain backdrop. Around 40 minutes' drive from the airport and a few bays south of the Al-Bustan Palace, the complex includes the Omani heritage village and *souk* (market), a 1,000-seat outdoor amphitheatre, 19 food outlets, pools, a lazy river, water-sports and a dive school, and a protected turtle nesting area.
PO Box 644, PC 113.
Tel: 24 776666.
Fax: 24 776677.
Email: slmu@shangri-la.com;
www.shangri-la.com

Sport and leisure
Bluzone Watersports Oman (Dive centre)
PADI Gold Palm resort with scuba courses of all levels and a four-day course for beginners. Pool and licensed restaurant.
Marina Bandar Al-Rowdah, PO Box 940, PC 113. Tel: 24 737293.
Email:
bluzone@omantel.net.om.
www.bluzonediving.com
Oman Dive Center
In its own peaceful bay, this is a PADI Gold Palm resort offering courses and dives, dolphin-watching tours and coastal cruises. There is a good licensed restaurant.
Tel: 24 824241. Email:
Muscat@extra-divers.li.
www.omandivecenter.com

Mina Al-Fahal
Accommodation
Oman Beach Hotel ★★★
A lovely quaint hotel close to the beach with rooms around the pool. There are 20 rooms and 20 suites, and an unlicensed restaurant.
PO Box 678, PC 116.
Tel: 24 696601. Fax: 24 6976686. Email: info@ omaninfobeachhotel.com

Muscat and Muttrah
ACCOMMODATION
Al-Mina Hotel ★
A basic hotel with 28
rooms on the Muttrah
corniche that has two
licensed restaurants,
one Indian and one
continental.
*PO Box 505, PC 112.
Tel: 24 711828. Fax: 24
714981. Email: minahotl
@omantel.net.om*
Corniche Hotel ★★
Good budget choice on
the Muttrah corniche
with 53 simple rooms, an
international restaurant
and friendly staff.
*PO Box 1800, PC 114.
Tel: 24 714707. Fax: 24
714770. Email: corniche_
hotel@mjsoman.com*
Marina Hotel ★★
A simple hotel on the
Muttrah corniche with
20 rooms, restaurant and
a bar on the roof terrace.
Excellent budget choice.
*PO Box 500, PC 114. Tel:
24 713100. Fax: 24
714666. Email: marina2@
omantel.net.om*
Al-Bustan Palace
Hotel ★★★★★
In a league of its own and
regularly voted top in the
Arabian Peninsula
competition, this hotel is
one of the finest in the
world. Set at one end of
its own sandy bay ringed
with dramatic mountains,
many people who come
here never set foot
beyond it. A complete
world within itself, the
hotel offers superb sports
facilities with tennis and
squash courts, gym, sauna
and massage parlour,
sailing, catamaran sailing
and windsurfing. The
swimming pool is huge
and there is a magnificent
sunbathing area with
palm trees and perfect
grass beside a children's
playground where the
swings face out to sea for
hours of reflective gazing.
There are eight
restaurants to choose
between, ranging from
gourmet to al fresco on
the beach. It has 250
rooms and over half of
these face the sea – you
can choose between
oriental décor with tiles
or continental. All rooms
have wireless internet
connection.
*PO Box 1998, Muscat
PC 114. Tel: 24 799666.
Fax: 24 799600. Email
albustan@interconti.com
or albustan@
albustanpalace.com.
www.albustanpalace.com*

EATING OUT
Kargeen Café ★★
One of three in the
Capital Area, all good,
but the best is in one of
the courtyards of the
Madinat Qaboos
Shopping Centre. It is
a traditional unlicensed
café with separate areas
for families, some tented,
some screened and
some open, creating a
unique oasis of Arabia
with smoking *shisha*
(water-pipe).
*Madinat Qaboos
Shopping Centre.
Tel: 24 692269.
www.kargeencaffe.com.
Open: 9.30am–3pm &
5pm–1am.*
Golden Dragon ★★★
In Madinat Qaboos
behind the shopping
complex, this licensed
Thai and Chinese
restaurant has attractive
décor and ambience.
*Tel: 24 697374.
Open: noon–3pm &
7–11.30pm.*
Purple Onion/
Al Inshirah ★★★
On the corniche by itself
between Muttrah and

Muscat opposite Riyam Park, this is now an Indian and Chinese restaurant serving good food.
Tel: 24 715482.
Lunch noon–3pm, dinner 7–midnight, Fri dinner only.

Al-Khiran Terrace ★★★★
An award-winning hotel buffet restaurant.
Al-Bustan Palace Hotel.
PO Box 1998, PC 114.
Tel: 24 799666.
Open for breakfast, lunch and dinner.
www.albustanpalace.com

ENTERTAINMENT
Al-Hamra (Nightclub)
Recently refurbished.
Al-Bustan Palace Hotel.
PO Box 1998, PC 114.
Tel: 24 799666.
www.albustanpalace.com

Marina Hotel Rooftop Bar
Marina Hotel,
Muttrah corniche.
PO Box 500, PC 114.
Tel: 24 713100.

Seblat Al-Bustan (Bar)
Traditional Omani music and dancing in a Bedouin tent accompanied by an Omani meal.
Al-Bustan Palace Hotel grounds. PO Box 1998,

PC 114. Tel: 24 799666.
www.albustanpalace.com

SPORT AND LEISURE
Muscat Golf Course
The first green 18-hole course.
PO Box 1040, PC 111.
Tel: 24 510065.
www.muscatgolf.com

Qurum and Ruwi
ACCOMMODATION
Al-Fanar Hotel ★
An unpretentious hotel with 48 rooms and an unlicensed restaurant.
PO Box 3738, PC 112.
Tel: 24 712385. Fax: 24 714994. Email:
alfanar@omantel.net.om

Qurum Beach Hotel ★★
A good location on Qurum Heights with lots of greenery around. This hotel is good value and has 64 rooms, an international restaurant and two nightclubs.
PO Box 2148, PC 112.
Tel: 24 564070. Fax: 24 560761. Email: qurum beachhotel@hotmail.com

Crowne Plaza Hotel ★★★
One of Muscat's oldest hotels, formerly the Gulf Forum, this boasts an excellent location on the cliff in Qurum Heights

overlooking Qurum Beach. There are 207 rooms, five restaurants, and very good sports and recreational facilities, including dive trips.
PO Box 1455, PC 112.
Tel: 24 560100,
24 660660. Fax: 24 560650, 24 574462.
Email: mcthc @intercontinenti.com.
www.cpmuscat.com

Ramada Qurum Hotel ★★★
Well located, close to the beach and the Intercontinental Hotel, the hotel has an Arabic-style design with 92 rooms. There is a restaurant and café.
PO Box 2994, PC 112. Tel: 24 603555. Fax: 24 694500. Email: ramadaom @omantel.net.om.
www.ramadamuscat.com

EATING OUT
Bellapais Restaurant ★★★
Licensed restaurant in the Rusail commercial complex serving Greek cuisine.
PO Box 82, PC 111.
Tel: 24 521100. Open: Sat–Thur noon–3pm & 6–11pm, Fri 6–11pm.

Mumtaz Mahal ★★★
Award-winning Indian restaurant on a hilltop overlooking Qurum Natural Park, probably the best place in the city. There is a good wine list. Enjoy the relaxing ambience with the waterfall backdrop.
Waterfall Hill, Qurum Natural Park.
Tel: 24 605907.
Open: noon–2.30pm & 7–11.30pm.

O Sole Mio ★★★
Located on Qurum Beach, this is an excellent Italian restaurant with a large wine list and a live Filipino band.
Qurum. Tel: 24 601343.
Open: Sat–Thur noon–4.45pm & 7–11pm, Fri 7–11pm.

Tokyo Taro ★★★
Eighth-floor Japanese restaurant.
Al-Falaj Hotel.
PO Box 3738, PC 112.
Tel: 24 712385.

Shiraz Lebanese Restaurant ★★★★
Persian cuisine.
Crowne Plaza Hotel.
PO Box 1455, PC 112.
Tel: 24 560100. Open for lunch and dinner.
www.cpmuscat.com

The Tuscany Italian Restaurant ★★★★
This restaurant is decorated as a re-creation of a Tuscan villa with gate and courtyard.
Grand Hyatt Hotel, Qurum Beach. Tel: 24 641234. Lunch noon–3.30pm, dinner 7–11.30pm, Fri dinner only.

ENTERTAINMENT
Al-Shatti Plaza (Cinema)
Films shown in English.
Qurum Beach. Open: 1.30pm–midnight.

Copacabana (Bar)
Brazilian-inspired interior.
Grand Hyatt Hotel, Qurum Beach.
Tel: 24 641234.

Duke's Bar
English pub.
Crowne Plaza Hotel.
PO Box 1455, PC 112.
Tel: 24 560100.
www.cpmuscat.com

John Barry Barat (Bar)
Named after the SS *John Barry*, which sank off the coast of Oman in 1944. The décor is nautical and the ambience quiet and upmarket, with a resident pianist.
Grand Hyatt Hotel, Qurum Beach.
Tel: 24 641234.

Ruwi Cinema
Films shown in English.
Mansoor Ali Shopping Centre. Tel: 24 780380. Open: 9am–1pm & 5–11pm.

Star Cinema
Films shown in English.
Bait Al Falaj Street.
Open: 2.30pm–12.30am.

SPORT AND LEISURE
Muscat Diving and Adventure Centre
Based on the beach in front of the Grand Hyatt, offering all the standard dive tours.
The Boat House, Grand Hyatt Hotel, Qurum Beach. Tel: 24 602101. Fax: 24 602542. Email: diveco@omantel.net.om. www.holiday-in-oman.com

Qurum Equestrian School
Qurum Natural Park.
Tel: 24 420444.

Sheraton Hotel (Bowling)
PO Box 3260, PC 112.

Seeb

ACCOMMODATION

Dream Resort ★★★

This hotel is near the beach, with rooms set around two pools. There are 30 rooms, a café lounge, an international restaurant and a nightclub.
PO Box 609, PC 121. Tel: 24 453399. Fax: 24 453999. Email: drmuscat @omantel.net.om or dreamr@omantel.net.om

SPORT AND LEISURE

Al-Sawahil Horse Riding

On the beach at Al-Bahja. Tel: 95 177557.

Oman Automobile Association (Motorsports)

Rents out go-karts, motorbikes, motocross/ dirt bikes, BMX bicycles, remote-controlled cars and skateboards.
Tel: 24 510239.

THE INTERIOR

Bahla

ACCOMMODATION

Bahla Hotel ★★

This is an extraordinary place found 2km (1¹/₄ miles) before Bahla proper. It has circular spaceship-like windows but six surprisingly large rooms with en-suite bathrooms in strange colours. There is a simple restaurant, which is unlicensed, but you can bring your own wine.
PO Box 187, PC 612. Tel: 25 420211. Fax: 25 420212.

Jebel Akhdar

ACCOMMODATION

Jebel Shams Travelling and Camping Centre ★

Six chalets and six tents with air-conditioning but no fridges or towels. Bring your own food.
Located at the top of the road to Jebel Shams from Wadi Ghul near Hamra. Tel: 24 635222.

Nizwa

ACCOMMODATION

Falaj Daris Hotel ★★

This mid-range hotel is a single-storey building set around two small pools. Licensed restaurant, bar and health club. The 55 rooms all have showers but no bath. There are no internet facilities.
PO Box 312, PC 611. Tel: 25 410500. Fax: 25 410537. Email: fdhnizwa@ omantel.net.om. www.falajdarishotel.com

Golden Tulip Hotel ★★

Formerly the Nizwa Motel, now owned by a Dutch hotel group, this is the most luxurious hotel in the interior, with cavernous communal areas and long corridors. There is a large pool, and the 120 comfortable rooms each have satellite TV and a minibar. There is a business centre, licensed restaurant, poolside café, lobby café and nightclub.
PO Box 1000, PC 611. Tel: 25 431616. Fax: 25 431619. Email: info@ goldentulipnizwa.co. www. goldentulipnizwa.com

Safari Hotel ★★

This hotel has 70 rooms, a pool, restaurant, bar and coffee shop.
PO Box 202, PC 611. Tel: 25 432150. Fax: 25 432151. Email: safariin@omantel.net.om

EATING OUT

Bin Ateeq ★

A traditional Omani unlicensed restaurant (*see p134*) with seating on cushions, this serves good-value food with dates and coffee rounding off the meal. The other two restaurants in the chain are in Muscat and Salalah.

Near Nizwa town centre and clearly signposted. Tel: 25 410466.

Al-Fanar ★★

Fully licensed restaurant serving a range of Indian, Chinese, continental and oriental dishes.

Falaj Daris Hotel. PO Box 312, PC 611. Tel: 25 410500.
www.falajdarishotel.com

Pizza Hut ★★

Spotlessly clean, open all day and with efficient air-conditioning, this can be just the place for homesick families desperate for some fast food. There is a salad bar and the usual pizzas – the only fast-food restaurant located in Oman's interior.

Tel: 25 412096.

Pool Café ★★

Poolside snack bar of the Golden Tulip Hotel that is also open to non-residents. This is a pleasant and tranquil setting in which to break your journey.

Golden Tulip Hotel. PO Box 1000, PC 611.
Tel: 25 431616. www. goldentulipnizwa.com

Birkat Al-Mawz Restaurant ★★★

Plush surroundings with an international menu and fully licensed.

Golden Tulip Hotel. PO Box 1000, PC 611. Tel: 25 431616. www. goldentulipnizwa.com

ENTERTAINMENT

Sahara Lounge

With belly dancing shows from 9pm.

Falaj Daris Hotel. PO Box 312, PC 611. Tel: 25 410500.
www.falajdarishotel.com

Tanuf Nightclub

Golden Tulip Hotel. IPO Box 1000, PC 611. Tel: 25 431616. www. goldentulipnizwa.com

SPORT AND LEISURE

There are opportunities for rock climbing, caving and trekking in the Jebel Akhdar (*see p144*).

Oman World Tourism

This tour operator can organise adventure trips and excursions – for more information visit *www. omanworldtourism.com*

THE BATINAH COAST
Barka

ACCOMMODATION

Al-Sawadi Beach Resort ★★★

A beautiful, restful hotel in its own lush grounds. There are 100 very comfortable rooms each with satellite TV and minibar. The large pool has a whirlpool and there is a children's playground, and paths lead onto the long, sandy beach with *barasti* (palm frond) sunshades. On the beach there are horse-riding stables and a diving school. From beach bar to nightclub, there are seven food outlets, all licensed. Tennis courts, fitness centre, water- sports and a business centre complete the resort.

PO Box 747, PC 320. Tel: 26 795545. Fax: 26 795535. Email: sales@alsawadibeach.com. www.alsawadibeach.com

Coral Al-Nahda Resort & Spa ★★★

Located in Barka within 12ha (30 acres) of gardens, this new luxury hotel is promoting itself as a health retreat with

gym and spa. There are 109 chalets.
North of Muscat on a rural, coastal site.
Tel: 26 883710. Fax: 26 883175. Email: stay@coral-alnahda.com

EATING OUT

Al-Sawadi Beach Resort ★★★
There are seven licensed restaurants serving Middle Eastern, classical, Continental and Asian food that can be used by non-residents.
PO Box 747, PC 320.
Tel: 26 795545.
Opening hours vary, call for information.
www.alsawadibeach.com

SPORT AND LEISURE

Al-Sawadi Beach Resort
Tennis courts, water-sports and health clubs, and a dive centre (*see below*). There are also stables on the beach offering horse-riding lessons and hacks.
PO Box 747, PC 320.
Tel: 26 795545.
www.alsawadibeach.com
Daymaniyat Divers Club
The only dive centre on the Batinah coast, this is a PADI Gold Palm resort

and National Geographic dive centre due to its commitment to marine conservation. There is a full range of courses and boat trips to the islands opposite, and all-inclusive packages are available with accommodation in the Al-Sawadi Beach Resort (*see p166*).
PO Box 747, PC 320.
Tel: 26 795545. Email: dive@alsawadibeach.com.
www.alsawadibeach.com

Sohar

ACCOMMODATION

Sohar Beach Hotel ★★
Designed like an Omani fort, painted white with four crenellated towers, the hotel sits on the beach in 4.5ha (11 acres) of landscaped gardens. A three-hour drive from Seeb International Airport or from Dubai International Airport, this makes a good stopping point midway between Muscat and Dubai. There are 40 rooms arranged on two storeys around the large pool, and there are good sports facilities. The four food outlets are all licensed.

PO Box 122, PC 321.
Tel: 26 841111.
Fax: 26 843766. Email: soharhtl@omantel.net.om.
www.soharbeach.com

EATING OUT

Alawi Al-Ghawi ★
Nicknamed Cute Ali, this simple unlicensed house of *barasti* (palm frond) serves rice with fish in a spicy sauce with onions, limes and lettuce, dates and water, followed by sweet herbal tea. There is traditional floor seating, a prayer room, and a fixed menu with low prices.
9km (5½ miles) north of Sohar roundabout on the coastal side of the dual carriageway.
Sohar Beach Hotel ★★★
There are four licensed food outlets here that can be used by non-residents – the Sallan Coffee Shop, Al Zafran night spot, and the Al Jizzi and the Al Taraif lounges.
PO Box 122, PC 321.
Tel: 26 841111.
www.soharbeach.com

ENTERTAINMENT

The only bars and nightclubs on the coast

are in the big hotels such as the Sawadi Beach Resort and the Sohar Beach Hotel.

SPORT AND LEISURE
Sohar Beach Hotel
Tennis courts, water-sports and health clubs.
PO Box 122, PC 321.
Tel: 26 841111.
www.soharbeach.com

MUSANDAM
Khasab
ACCOMMODATION
Golden Tulip Resort ★★
By far the best place to stay in Musandam, and the only place with a licensed restaurant, this hotel has 60 rooms. The resort organises special boat trips to Telegraph Island and tours into the mountains by four-wheel drive.
PO Box 434, PC 811.
Tel: 26 730777. Fax: 26 730888. Email: info@ goldentulipkhasab.com. www.goldentulipkhasab. com
Khasab Hotel ★★
Located inland from the town, this is a simple hotel and the first to be built in Musandam. There are 15 rooms laid

out around the pool, and an unlicensed restaurant.
PO Box 111, PC 811.
Tel: 26 730267. Fax: 26 730989. Email: khoman@ omantel.net.om. Accepts cash only.

EATING OUT
Khasab Hotel Restaurant ★★
A simple place, unlicensed, but you can bring your own wine. The food has an international flavour.
PO Box 111, PC 811.
Tel: 26 730267.
Dibba Restaurant ★★★
The only licensed restaurant in Musandam. serving international fare.
Golden Tulip Resort. PO Box 434, PC 811.
Tel: 26 730777. www. goldentulipkhasab.com

SPORT AND LEISURE
Extra Divers & Partners
This outfit offers courses, dives and trips aboard traditional dhows into the 'fjords' (*see p84*).
Operating from the Golden Tulip Resort. PO Box 434, PC 811. Tel: 26 730501. Email: musandam@extra-divers.li. www.extra-divers.li

Khasab Travel & Tours
A range of trips from half a day to three days into the mountains, and on dhows for dolphin-watching excursions.
PO Box 50, PC 811.
Tel: 26 730464. Email: khastour@omantel.net.om. www.khasabtours.com

EASTERN PROVINCE (SHARQIYAH)
Al-Mudayrib
ACCOMMODATION
Al-'Areesh Desert Camp ★★
The camp is just south of Al-Mudayrib and comprises a group of 43 tent bungalows covered in *barasti* (palm frond) with lighting and bedding, and a shower/toilet block. The camp is used by tour groups and there is dune driving, camel rides and sand-skiing.
Tel: 24 493232.
Email: tours@omantel. net.om. www.desert-discovery.com
Al-Qabil Resthouse ★★
Simple, good-value resthouse just beyond Al-Mudayrib with 10 rooms. Each room has a fridge, TV, air-conditioning and room

service. There is an unlicensed restaurant but there is a bar.
PO Box 53, PC 419.
Tel: 25 581243.
Fax: 25 581119.

SPORT AND LEISURE
Al-'Areesh Desert Camp
Tours into the Wahhiba Sands (*see p104*) by four-wheel drive with drivers and guides.

Al-Wasil
ACCOMMODATION
Golden Sands Camp ★★
This offers better accommodation than the other camps, with 20 en-suite chalets. There are children's activities such as archery, quad bikes and an adventure playground.
Tel: 99 445092.

Bidiyah
ACCOMMODATION
Oriental Nights Rest House ★★★★
A small, simple hotel near Al-Mintirib set in gardens of mango and orange trees. The 19 rooms have room service, and the hotel is popular with Europeans as it is by far the most Westernised place around.

PO Box 84, PC 421.
Tel: 99 354816.
Fax: 24 493836.
Email: onrh@onrh.net.
www.onrh.net

SPORT AND LEISURE
Oriental Nights Rest House
Tours into the Wahhiba Sands by four-wheel drive are run every Thursday.
PO Box 84, PC 421. Tel: 99 354816. www.onrh.net

Ibra
ACCOMMODATION
Al-Sharqiya Sands Hotel ★★
An attractive hotel halfway between Muscat and Sur, with a garden courtyard and pool (a rarity in this area). There are 24 rooms, a licensed international restaurant and a pub.
PO Box 585, PC 413.
Tel: 99 205112.
Fax: 99 207012. Email: moktil@rediffmail.com
Nahar Tourism Farm Camp ★★
The camp has six *barasti* (palm frond) huts in Wadi Nam near Ibra, clearly signposted. Run by an enterprising local Omani, this charming

collection of huts offers a different kind of experience, with generators for lighting and no air-conditioning. There is a basic shower and toilet block. The price includes breakfast and a barbecued evening meal but is still severely overpriced. You can bring your own alcohol.
PO Box 9, PC 115. Tel: 99 387654. Fax: 24 698292.
Email: emptyqtr @omantel.net.om. www. emptyquartertours.com

SPORT AND LEISURE
Nahar Tourism Farm Camp
Tours arranged into the Wahhiba Sands by four-wheel drive (self-drive or guided).
PO Box 9, PC 115.
Tel: 99 387654. www. emptyquartertours.com

Sur
ACCOMMODATION
Ras Al-Hadd Beach Hotel ★★
Part of the Sur group of hotels, there are 50 rooms, a licensed international restaurant and bar. The hotel arranges turtle tours and permits.

PO Box 400, PC 411. Tel: 99 376989. Fax: 99 314002. Email: surbhtl@omantel.net.om

Sur Beach Hotel ★★

Unexciting but comfortable hotel on the beach en route to Ras Al-Hadd. There are 188 rooms, a pool, a licensed restaurant, a bar with live music, and a coffee shop. *PO Box 400, PC 411. Tel: 25 542031. Fax: 25 542228. Email: surbhtl@omantel.net.om. www.sigoh.com.om*

Sur Plaza Hotel ★★

Set inland with no pool, the hotel has 102 rooms, a licensed restaurant and two bars with live entertainment. *PO Box 908, PC 411. Tel: 25 543777. Fax: 25 542626. Email: resvnsur @omanhotels.com. www. omanhotels.com/sur.htm*

Turtle Beach Resort ★★

Twenty-two traditional beach huts 8km (5 miles) beyond Ras Al-Hadd town. The resort has a private beach, a dhow-shaped restaurant and can arrange turtle- and dolphin-watching tours. The room price includes breakfast and dinner.

PO Box 303, PC 411. Tel: 25 540068. Fax: 25 543900. Email: surtour@omantel.net. www.surtoursonline.com/ resort.htm

EATING OUT

The only places to eat in the Eastern Province (Sharqiyah) are in the simple coffee shops in and around Ibra and in Sur. Those at Sur are licensed. Outside the hotels, the most you will find are some simple Indian road-side places.

ENTERTAINMENT

The bars of the Sur Plaza and Sur Beach have live music.

SPORT AND LEISURE

Ras Al-Hadd Beach Hotel

Excursions to see turtles (*see p99*) and dolphins can be arranged. *PO Box 400, PC 411. Tel: 99 376989. Email: surbhtl@omantel.net.om*

Turtle Beach Resort

Turtle tours and dolphin-watching. *PO Box 303, PC 411. Tel: 25 540068. www.surtoursonline.com/ resort.htm*

DHOFAR
Salalah
ACCOMMODATION

Haffa House Hotel ★★

The hotel has 63 rooms arranged as one-, two- or three-bed apartments. There are sports facilities, a restaurant and an English tearoom. *PO Box 427, PC 211. Tel: 23 295444. Fax: 23 294873. Email: house@omantel.net.om*

Salalah Beach Villas ★★

This establishment offers 25 rooms, 10 apartments, and 8 beach villas. Tours can be arranged with a prepared picnic. *PO Box 20, PC 214, Dahariz. Tel: 23 235999. Fax: 23 235599. Email: beachspa@omantel.net.om*

Samharam Tourist Village ★★

Close to the Hilton (*see opposite*), this is a peaceful beachfront resort with 46 villas and 16 chalets. There is a pool, restaurant and café. *PO Box 427, PC 211. Tel: 23 295444. Fax: 23 211267.*

Crowne Plaza Resort ★★★

Directly on the beach, the resort has 153 rooms, a

large pool, a health club with sauna, a whirlpool and a gym. There is a nine-hole golf course and three licensed restaurants.
PO Box 870, PC 211. Tel: 23 235333. Fax: 23 235137. Email: cpsll@ omantel.net.om. www. crowneplaza.com/salalah

Hilton Salalah Resort ★★★

This resort has 150 rooms, a pool and sports facilities, two licensed restaurants, a beach café, an English pub and a nightclub.
PO Box 699, PC 211. Tel: 23 211234. Fax: 23 210084. Email: salalah@ hilton.com. www.salalah.hilton.com

EATING OUT

Bin Ateeq ★

This is one of three unlicensed restaurants of excellent value. The others are in Muscat and Nizwa. Traditional Omani food is served.
Salalah. Tel: 23 292384. Email: binateeq@ omantel.net.om

Al-Khareef ★★

This pub serves hot and cold bar food.
Crowne Plaza Resort. PO Box 870, PC 211.

Tel: 23 235333. Open for lunch and dinner. www. crowneplaza.com/salalah

Al-Maha ★★★

Inside the Hilton Salalah Resort, this licensed restaurant serves Arabian and international cuisine.
PO Box 699, PC 211. Tel: 23 211234. Open: daily 6.30am–10.30pm. www.salalah.hilton.com

Darbat ★★★

Inside the Crowne Plaza Resort, this licensed restaurant serves breakfast, lunch and dinner. There is a terrace overlooking the sea.
Crowne Plaza Resort. PO Box 870, PC 211. Tel: 23 235333. www. crowneplaza.com/salalah

Palm Grove ★★★

This licensed restaurant in the Hilton Salalah Resort serves fresh fish.
PO Box 699, PC 211. Tel: 23 211234. Open: daily noon–10.30pm. www.salalah.hilton.com

ENTERTAINMENT

Al-Khareef (Bar)

Pub serving cocktails.
Crowne Plaza Resort. PO Box 870, PC 211. Tel: 23 235333. www. crowneplaza.com/salalah

Sunset Lounge (Bar)

Bar with widescreen TV.
Hilton Salalah Resort. PO Box 699, PC 211. Tel: 23 211234. www.salalah.hilton.com

Whispers (Nightclub)

Live music and dance.
Hilton Salalah Resort. PO Box 699, PC 211. Tel: 23 211234. www.salalah.hilton.com

SPORT AND LEISURE

Crowne Plaza Resort

This hotel boasts tennis and health clubs, a nine-hole green golf course, its own dive centre and boat trips with shark-fishing. Also lays on four-wheel drive tours into the Empty Quarter and to Ubar (*see pp118–19*), and frankincense tours to the west of Salalah (*see p112*).
Crowne Plaza Resort. PO Box 870, PC 211. Tel: 23 235333. www. crowneplaza.com/salalah

Hilton Salalah Resort

Tennis and health clubs, and four-wheel drive tours into the Empty Quarter. Also half-day frankincense trail tours.
PO Box 699, PC 211. Tel: 23 211234. www.salalah.hilton.com

Index

Acknowledgements

Thomas Cook wishes to thank the photographer, DIANA DARKE, for the loan of the photographs reproduced in this book, to whom copyright in the photographs belongs (except the following):
ARABIAN ORYX SANCTUARY 110
CHRISTINE OSBORNE PICTURES112
DREAMSTIME.COM 1 (Marc Johnson), 125 (Nasser Bu-hamad)
HANS ROSSEL 139
MIKE KRAMER 138
PHOTOSHOT/EYE UBIQUITOUS 147
PICTURES COLOUR LIBRARY 115
SHANGRI-LA 137
WIKIMEDIA COMMONS 83 (Eckhard Pecher), 100, 101 (Bertil Videt), 113 (snotch), 116
WORLD PICTURES 131 (Jenny Fowler), 141

For CAMBRIDGE PUBLISHING MANAGEMENT LTD:
Project editor: Tom Lee
Typesetter: Donna Pedley
Proofreader: Jan McCann
Indexer: Karolin Thomas

SEND YOUR THOUGHTS TO
BOOKS@THOMASCOOK.COM

We're committed to providing the very best up-to-date information in our travel guides and constantly strive to make them as useful as they can be. You can help us to improve future editions by letting us have your feedback. If you've made a wonderful discovery on your travels that we don't already feature, if you'd like to inform us about recent changes to anything that we do include, or if you simply want to let us know your thoughts about this guidebook and how we can make it even better – we'd love to hear from you.

Send us ideas, discoveries and recommendations today and then look out for your valuable input in the next edition of this title.

Emails to the above address, or letters to Travellers Series Editor, Thomas Cook Publishing, PO Box 227, Coningsby Road, Peterborough PE3 8SB, UK.

Please don't forget to let us know which title your feedback refers to!